LIFE AFTER THE DEATH OF MY SON

LIFE AFTER THE DEATH OF MY SON

WHAT I'M LEARNING

DENNIS L. APPLE

BEACON HILL PRESS
OF KANSAS CITY

Copyright 2008
By Dennis L. Apple and Beacon Hill Press of Kansas City

ISBN 978-0-8341-2365-6

Printed in the
United States of America

Cover Design: Brandon Hill
Internal Design: Sharon Page

Library of Congress Cataloging-in-Publication Data

Apple, Dennis, 1942-
  Life after the death of my son : what I'm learning / Dennis Apple.
    p. cm.
  ISBN-13: 978-0-8341-2365-6 (pbk.)
  ISBN-10: 0-8341-2365-7 (pbk.)
  1. Children—Death—Religious aspects—Christianity. 2. Bereavement—Religious aspects—Christianity. 4. Fathers—Religious life. 5. Apple, Dennis, 1942- I. Title.

  BV4907.A57 2008
  248.8'66—dc22

                                    2008000148

10 9 8 7 6 5 4 3

CONTENTS

INTRODUCTION

Our son, Denny Apple, died February 6, 1991. I discovered his lifeless body in our family room at 8:20 A.M. We will never be the same. We do not know the exact reason for his death. The coroner's report simply reads, "Complications due to mono."

I recall the day after Denny's death and the strange compulsion I had to begin journaling. I had no idea where it would lead me, but I knew I must write about the nightmare our family was experiencing. I knew it had to be expressed in some way, or I would die. So at the end of each day, after brushing my teeth and preparing for bed, before turning off the lights, I reached for my notebook and pen from the nightstand. I always dated my journal entries and usually entered the time as well.

I usually made my entries around 11:00 P.M., often as my wife, Buelah, cried herself to sleep. I poured out my helplessness, frustration, and unspeakable pain. For nearly five years I continued this bedtime ritual. After filling a notebook, I would take it to a storage closet and add it to the growing stack. The notebooks gathered dust in the darkness for 10 years.

Then, last summer, my friend Harold Ivan Smith and I were sitting in a Mexican restaurant. I was startled when he looked directly at me and said, "Dennis, now that you've been on this journey for 15 years, I think there's something you need to say to other parents who are just beginning their grief journeys. Why don't you write down the 10 most important things you've learned and share it with other parents in a book?" I thought it was a ridiculous idea at first. But he wouldn't take no for an answer.

I finally agreed to write, and that meant going back into the storage closet, dusting off the journals, and reliving the nightmare I had tried so hard to forget. It was a formidable task to read through the pain of my personal train wreck, to experience again the helplessness and despair that comes from losing a child. There were times I could read only a small portion. However, as I continued to read through the pages and make notations, it became easier.

At the beginning of each chapter I have included a journal entry that illustrates the lesson I learned. You will find other journal entries in each chapter as well. The thoughts and feelings recorded in these journals are honest and sometimes gut-wrenching. However, I have made no attempt to clean up or sanitize them. What you see here is the raw, uncut, and uncensored version of a grieving man who is trying to stay alive by pouring out his pain.

The United States Army uses the term "ground

truth" to describe the real experience of soldiers in the field—the moment-by-moment truth of being in combat as opposed to generalizations about combat or theories about how it *should* occur. Here in these pages you will find excerpts from my journal—and some from my wife's—that describe the way it really happened for me and my family. Our son Andrew, Denny's younger brother, also has a poem included as well.

My reason for writing this book is to give grieving parents hope. In some ways, I feel like an African guide on a wildlife safari. I'll point out some of the wild animals to stay away from, trails to take or avoid, and suggestions for hacking your way through the weeds and vines that spring up in front of you.

You *can* survive the death of your child. You *can*, with God's help, redeem this disaster and turn it into something that will make a difference in the world. As you do, you'll see how God can continue the life of the child you loved and lost.

ONE

WILL IT ALWAYS HURT THIS MUCH?

4/15/95

A long day that should have been happy but instead is filled with sadness, depression, and tears. I don't know if I can continue to live this way. Not only have I lost a son, but I have lost a wife as well. She turns down all offers of suggestions for help and claims she is OK. Yet her face and actions tell another story. It is hard to stand by and watch a person deteriorate like this. She has no hope—no goals—nothing to live for, and the love is slowly leaving. It's funny how I give my life to help others and yet I cannot help my own wife, nor does she want help from me or any other person. I wonder how long we will continue like this.

My wife and I walked into the small, smoke-filled room where the support group was meeting. It had been only two weeks since our son had suddenly died. We were in deep shock, going through each day as if we were zombies, hoping we would wake up from this nightmare.

After the meeting, I met with some of the men while Buelah visited with the women. All of us had one thing in common: we had lost a child by death. They asked us how long it had been, and we numbly told them it had been two weeks. Then one of the women spoke up and said to us, "Hang in there—the second year is often worse than the first!" I remember thinking, *If that's true, then you might as well go ahead and kill us right now. There's no way we'll make it if it gets any worse than this.*

Looking back, I see that she was trying to prepare us. Much of our first year was spent in a daze as we trudged through each day like sad robots. It was a surreal experience, something like waking up after having a general anesthetic. On one level you know you're awake, and you can hear what the nurse is saying to you. On another level you're still in a fog and will need assistance for several hours. Parents who have lost a child are in this fog for years, not just hours or days.

Fresh grievers don't want to hear this truth, but it's best to be prepared for what's to come and to also be reassured that good news will come later in this journey. The first year was indeed spent in mind-numbing shock.

We both thought we were living our worst nightmare and hoped we would soon wake up and find out it was caused by the pizza we ate the night before. When we faced the second year, the second round of painful reminders on the calendar, we knew we were in this for the long haul.

When a runner is preparing for a race, it's important for him or her to know the distance of the race. The distance determines the runner's mind-set, preparation, and the strategy for completing the race. In a short race, there's no need to stop for water—it will be over in a few seconds or minutes. A marathon, on the other hand, requires careful planning. The runner dares not pass those important water stops.

My journal entry of April 15, 1995, may have led you to believe that our son had died only a few weeks earlier. But it's a snapshot of the struggles we were having a full four years after Denny's death. In those days I was weary and running low on hope. I came very close to giving in to my despair. In my office at church, I listened as an increasing number of people came to me to share their own experiences of pain and loss. I listened to those who were grieving the loss of a child, spouse, parent, sibling, or grandparent. I stepped into stories of unemployment, loss of friendships, and even terminal illness as some were starting the process of grieving their own deaths.

13

People seemed to know instinctively that my deep loss had somehow brought me to the place at which I might understand and sympathize with their loss. I identified with Rabbi Harold Kushner, the author of *When Bad Things Happen to Good People*. People told him he was a much better speaker, counselor, and writer after the death of his son. In those days, people often left my office with appreciative tears in their eyes, knowing someone had really listened to them. I was becoming aware that the brokenness of my heart somehow resonated with the broken people sitting in front of me.

My ministry was taking a different direction, and I knew that somehow God was taking my sorrow and using it to help others as they mourned their own losses. I was glad to be of comfort, but I wanted to move more quickly beyond my pain.

I longed to help my family so they, too, could move past the pain. Yet when I went home and tried to "fix" my wife, she resisted my pastoral counseling techniques. She continued with her determined depression, day after day, month after month, year after year.

At times it felt as though we were chained together on some sort of death march, much like the stories that came from the prisoners of war in World War II. They were often deprived of food and water and had to deal with frostbite and illness. Yet they were forced to continue their long march until they either fell and died or reached their destination. Bereaved parents feel as though they're on a long, sad march but have no final destination. We feel as though this overwhelming sadness will be with us forever.

We're expected to move on, yet something within us resists these expectations to move on so quickly. A good analogy might be a high-priced professional athlete who's expected to play in an important game. He or she is hurt but is taped up and sometimes drugged to make it possible to continue participating, even though he or she really should not be competing. We fans know the athlete is hurt and can sometimes see blood seeping through the bandages, and we applaud the bravado of the fierce competitor who plays through injuries.

Bereaved parents are also learning how to play hurt, but the casual onlooker has no idea how badly they've been injured or how long it will take to recover.

Perhaps we should return to the days when bereaved persons wore black armbands or displayed symbols in their front windows that indicated a death in the family. On Ash Wednesday the priest or minister takes ashes and carefully makes the sign of the Cross on our foreheads. We want all to see—for a day—that we Christians are a people of the Cross, living between Good Friday and Easter Sunday.

For the newly bereaved parent, though, every day feels like Ash Wednesday, and we want everyone to see and understand the devastation of our loss.

Yes, bereaved parents learn how to play hurt.

Our injury is made even worse by people who try to fast-forward us through our grief. They suggest we should come to some sort of closure. In my attempt to ward off the shallow words from those who spoke about closure, I borrowed a phrase from another griever whom I heard say, "People close on houses, not the death of a child."

I found a better word that more accurately described the task before me—to *reconcile* myself to my son's death.

I suppose I first noticed this word, *reconcile*, just after I opened my first checking account as a young adult. After the first month, I received a statement from the bank with instructions about the importance of reconciling my checkbook to the bank statement. It was imperative that my checkbook reflect the same balance as the one on the bank's statement.

In order to reconcile myself to Denny's death, I had to go through the process of reconciling my heart—not my head—to the reality of his death. I had no idea of the amount of time this process would take for me and my family. Looking back over my "before Denny's death" years (BDD) as a pastor, I recall several times when I looked into the sad eyes of someone who had lost a child by death and wondered why he or she was having such a hard time recovering from the loss. I'm quite sure I said some things that sounded very pastoral but served only to hurt or cause the grieving parents to question their own sanity as they tried to come to terms with their painful loss.

By the way, I have already asked God to forgive me for the hurry-up-and-get-over-it words I spoke to countless grievers I encountered during the early years of my ministry. I wish I could take back those words. Perhaps this book will help educate and sensitize people to the length of time it takes for a parent to valiantly reclaim his or her life.

Few people whose children are all living understand the formidable task that bereaved parents face. Gradually, bereaved parents must face the realization that their lives, and the lives of their entire family, have been changed forever. The struggle before them is to find a new "normal."

One of the biggest lies a griever hears is that time heals all wounds. How I wish this were true! It isn't. Time is important, but time alone will not heal a broken heart. In my journey, it has taken time plus the company of others who acknowledged my pain and hopelessness.

During these past 16 years I have noticed some of the important factors that affect a griever's journey:

- Your relationship with the child
- The circumstances surrounding the child's death
- The age of the child
- The support of family and friends.

Your Relationship with the Child

I enjoyed a very close relationship with Denny. When he was born, I was fresh out of seminary and pastoring a small church in the south suburbs of Chicago that averaged about 50 worshipers on Sunday mornings. The church and parsonage were physically connected, so our living quarters, the place of worship, and my office were all under one roof. It was very convenient, especially in the winter time. In order to attend the worship services, we just walked downstairs, through the basement, and up to the sanctuary on the other side. My office was also near the sanctuary, so this arrangement allowed me to stay close to my wife and help out in those early days after Denny's birth.

When Buelah needed a break, I just left the office, walked a few feet down the hallway, and gave her a hand. I had a lot of experience helping raise my nine younger brothers and sisters, and I was comfortable with preparing the formula and feeding our son, changing diapers, and giving baths. All of this allowed me to bond with

Denny in a very special way. I imagine those early days together helped forge my strong relationship with him. Our family photo albums hold scores of pictures of us together, often with me down on all fours, giving him horsey rides and playing on the floor together. One picture shows the two of us holding a five-pound catfish we caught together. In that picture he is about four years old, and one can see the admiring look in his eyes as we shared that special moment with each other.

As he grew up, I made it a priority to attend every football, basketball, and baseball game, often as his coach but always as his biggest fan. Later, when he reached the early years of adolescence, a time when children tend to pull away from their parents, he often walked close to me, even in public places such as the shopping mall, holding my hand as we walked along together. I felt a bit uncomfortable holding the hand of my 13-year-old son in public and would often release his hand and reach up and rest my hand on his shoulder. Somehow that felt more manly than holding hands.

Across the years I've heard heartbreaking stories of parents who told me the very last conversation they had with their child was filled with words of anger and rage. They confessed they would give anything to have those moments back to do things differently. Their grief is complicated by the layer of regret that's added to their already painful recovery. Sometimes an understanding friend or trained therapist can assist a griever as he or she works through those haunting memories. The Bible is wise on this point as we are encouraged in Eph. 4:26 not to let the sun go down while we're still angry.

In the years since Denny's death, I've had several grieving parents ask me how long they'll feel so devastated or how long it will be until they feel like living again. I tell them that I wish I could fast-forward them through their upcoming pain and suffering. I want to tell them it will be over with soon—but I'm reluctant to give anyone a specific time as a reference point for his or her grief. We're all different, and many factors affect the amount of time it takes.

In our case, it was nearly five years before we wanted to pick up the pieces and go on with our lives. As you look back over my journal entry, you can see the homesickness I had for Denny as you read the words from October 13, 1992:

I don't know why, but something triggered my thoughts about him. I just miss him and can feel his skin, his closeness, his hair, his scalp, I can almost sense his closeness tonight . . . and it is killing me. Oh, how I long to hold him again and tell him I love him and hear his words, "I love you too, Dad." Oh, how can

I go on when my heart has been torn from me? Oh, God—I'm still asking "Why?"

These words were written more than 18 months after Denny's death, and I'm certain there were those who were close to me who would be shocked to know that this is what I was feeling at that time.

My wife and I each had a wonderful relationship with Denny. He often came home from school and, finding his mother in the kitchen, grabbed her and danced with her. I could hear them laughing as he dipped her back until her long hair swept across the floor. He had a very special relationship with her. When he was in elementary school, he took pride in the fact that his mom was the room mother. He loved having her on the field trips and always found a way to sit next to her on the bus.

Later, when he started driving, he often came to our bedroom when he returned home from a date or a night out with his buddies. Before going to his room, he would knock on our bedroom door and ask if he could come in. He would sit on the edge of the bed and spend several minutes with us, sharing the interesting things that had happened during his day. Before he left the room, he tucked the covers in around our chins and whispered, "You're the best parents in the whole world." He would kiss each of us on the forehead and then quietly slip off to his room. He was a very affectionate young man who was comfortable with hugs and kisses.

Denny had obviously learned this bedtime ritual from us. When he was very young, we had established the nightly ritual of tucking him under the covers and whispering that he was a wonderful son and that we were very proud of him. As he was slipping off to sleep, we wanted him to hear our words of love and confidence in him. I wish we could have said our good-byes to him the night he died!

Circumstances Surrounding the Child's Death

Sometimes a child's death is preceded by months or years of chemotherapy, radiation, or other forms of therapy, as the parents watch the life of their precious child slowly ebb away. I've sat with anxious parents in hospital waiting rooms as they awaited the outcome of a long surgery on their child. My heart went out to them as I heard "Oh, my God!" screams as the surgeon grimly told them that their child had six months to a year to live. Their grief journey had begun. As they clung to hope and prayed for a cure, they also prepared themselves to say good-bye.

Sometimes it comes suddenly. While I served as a chaplain to state troopers, we knocked on the door and delivered the news no parent ever wants to hear: "Your child is dead." Watching a parent go into shock is one of the hardest things to witness.

Two days before I discovered Denny's body, I had taken him to the doctor, and we had been told he had mononucleosis. Medications were prescribed, and he was advised to rest and let his body recover. We were planning to leave on a ski trip in two days, and the doctor said Denny could make the trip but probably wouldn't feel much like skiing. The night he died, Denny wanted to sleep on the couch near the fireplace and television set. On February 6, just after taking our younger son to school, I found him. That memory is seared into my mind forever.

My journal entry of February 25, 1991, reveals what it was like for me.

I try to forget and even deny that he is gone, but the whole scene of finding him is firmly in my mind. To think I walked right past the couch and into the garage when I took Andy to school. It was very foggy, and Andy mentioned how hard Denny was breathing as he studied at the kitchen table the night before. I came back home, had a bowl of cereal, but could not hear Denny breathing on the couch as he lay there, about 12 feet away. I thought he must have turned the corner, he must be better—he isn't breathing hard like he did last night. He will enjoy the ski trip more.

I went down to the family room, looked at his neck because I thought he was very still—I get closer—maybe I touched his arm—(this is too much to write about here). . . . I yell to Buelah, who is coming up the stairs from the laundry room, "He's not breathing! Call 911!" I instinctively try CPR. I scream for Scott—he is an EMT. He comes quickly and tries to listen for a heartbeat. Buelah is crying and screaming into the phone. Scott throws up his hands and says, "Dennis, it's too late. He's gone!" I scream, "This isn't supposed to happen to me, God! Where are you?" NIGHTMARE!

As I write these words, 16 years later, the hair still stands up on the back of my neck, and my heart rate increases as I allow myself to feel the horror of it all over again.

There are other factors that affect our grief journey. The child may have been murdered or chosen to take his or her own life. There may be unanswered questions and court hearings that add to the overwhelming pain a parent is already suffering.

Soon after my son died, a young teenage girl from our church was abducted as she spoke with her boyfriend from a pay telephone. Her last words were screams for help as the line went silent. Now, after 16 years, she has never been heard from, and her parents have sadly reached the conclusion that she is dead. Her dad shared with me that he still hopes she has amnesia and that someday she'll walk through the door and back to her waiting family. Through the years he has struggled between hanging onto hope and grieving her death.

Age of the Child

I have served in what some would call a mega-church for more than 20 years and have stood with several parents who have suffered the death of a child. Some children died even before they were born, while others were well into their 40s or older, often leaving behind grandchildren for the grieving parents.

I have grieved with those whose children didn't live long enough for a parent-child relationship to develop. Their grief is a bit different as they mourn the death of dreams and a future that will never be. I recall the words of a loving grandmother as she tucked the soft blanket under the chin of her beautiful, stillborn granddaughter just before the casket was closed. Through her tears she said, "It wasn't supposed to be like this."

Obviously, this grandmother, along with the child's parents, will always grieve the child they never got to know and will always wonder what it might have been like to watch her grow up, take her first step, start school, attend her first prom, get married, have children. They feel as though someone broke into their lives and robbed them of their most precious possession.

All these factors and others affect the length of time it takes a parent to struggle and reconcile to a child's death. This is one of the reasons it's not wise to say, "I know just how you feel, because I also lost a child." One never knows the heart of the relationship another has with his or her child.

Support of Family and Friends

I often counsel grieving parents who say that other members of their family feel they should be "over it by now." Grieving parents feel anger and resentment toward those who are trying to push them to a quick resolution of their grief. Often I have the task of trying to help the person in front of me and also educate the other family members, helping them understand the magnitude of this loss and the time it will take to recover.

Buelah, Andy, and I were very fortunate that our entire family was very supportive of us. I'm the oldest of 10 children, and they rushed to my side when they heard the news of Denny's death. They cried with me and, to this day, continue to share their memories of Denny with me. As I think of all the ways they supported us, I'll never forget that special prayer they had for us the day after the funeral. Before they returned to their respective homes, we all stood together in our living room, and Bev led our family in asking God to give us "time-released" comfort over the next days and weeks to come. Later my sister Jeanette also lost her precious child, Megan, and once again the family moved quickly to her side, like EMTs rushing to a horrible accident. Buelah and I are blessed to have the unwavering support of our wonderful families.

Even with all of the support that's available, there are times when a bereaved parent feels as though he or she has hit a wall. Marathon runners know about "hitting the wall." This is the result of a build-up of lactic acid in the leg muscles, and it usually occurs around the 20th mile. The runner often feels as if an extra 50 pounds of concrete is strapped to his or her legs. Running through this pain requires almost superhuman effort. The water stops and cheers from the sidelines become especially important as sweat-soaked, weary runners try to find the courage to ignore their pain and press on to the finish line.

Bereaved parents need to know where their water stops are located. They need to know what messages to listen to from the sidelines. They need to know they can survive this grueling trip they never intended to take. In a word, they need to find hope that they can survive their nightmare. My goal is that this book will help you face the journey toward your "new normal." Be patient with yourself. This trip will take longer than you think!

TWO

WILL OUR MARRIAGE SURVIVE THIS?

3/23/91

I took Buelah out for breakfast and tried to cheer her up. She is so sad and cries often. I don't know what to do! I mourn differently than she does—and yet I feel she expects me to cry and be depressed like she is. I don't know—maybe I'm not in touch with my own feelings.

I'm disturbed today because Buelah and I seem to be more apart emotionally than we've been in a long time. I'm not sure why except that we're handling this whole thing differently. Perhaps tomorrow will be different.

On June 6, 1964, I stood at the altar of our church, looking into the eyes of my beautiful bride, and repeated after the minister, "I promise to love, honor, and keep her, in sickness and health and, forsaking all others, keep myself only unto her, for as long as I live." Looking back,

I think perhaps the ceremony should have included the words "Even if we lose a child by death, I will still stand by her."

As I write these lines, I can honestly say these are some of the best days of our marriage. We spend as much of each day together as possible. We joke around and laugh more now than at any other time in our marriage. It wasn't always this way. In the months and years following our son's death, there were times when we thought about going our separate ways. We still loved each other, but the grief from our son's death was like a dirty wedge, driving us apart.

It was only a few days after Denny died when we heard about a special grief seminar that was to be held near where we live. We made plans to attend and listened carefully as the speaker addressed grief and mourning. He pointed out that there's a difference between the two.

Grief, according to him, was like a large stone tied to your heart. Grief is a feeling you carry inside, a heaviness of spirit.

Mourning, on the other hand, is best described as putting the grief on the outside. Mourning is the public expression of grief. Signs of mourning are crying, sad conversation, sad countenance of the face and body.

One of the points he made stuck with me and has

proven to be painfully true: "Women mourn, but men replace." This is a general statement about the ways men and women mourn in North America. It seemed to be true for us as well.

The first few days after Denny's death were filled with deep anguish and tears from both of us. After two weeks, I intentionally dried up my tears and went back to work while she still mourned alone at home. As a man, I felt I should be the strong one, the provider and protector. As I look back, I realize I was starting to replace my deepest pain with the busyness of my daily work schedule.

I recall several mornings when we awakened and sat on our respective sides of the bed. Then, from the other side of the bed, I would hear a sad sigh, like a weary mountain climber picking up her heavy backpack and preparing to climb Mount Everest after a sleepless night. I would hurry in to shower, shave, and dress for the day, trying to avoid looking at her sad face.

Soon after, I would be in the car, the radio on as I drove the eight blocks to my office at the church. At my desk, I structured the day so that it was filled with phone calls, appointments, hospital visitation, and e-mail. Reading books or magazines was out of the question, since my comprehension was practically zero. I made certain my days were filled with noise and activity. If I allowed even the smallest amount of silence to occur, thoughts of finding Denny dead on the couch came crashing into my mind like an avalanche. I used noise and activity to keep my mind from replaying that nightmare.

Across the years I have met countless men and women who have used drugs, alcohol, sex, food, gambling, work, hobbies, or shopping to drown out the painful scenes in their minds. My drug of choice was work. My hectic schedule was a convenient distraction, and it was something I used in my attempt to outrun the pain.

At the end of the day, when I returned home from the office, I found Buelah much the same as I had left her in the morning. Her sad, puffy eyes gave evidence of a long day of crying. Her beautiful hair would be unkempt, her voice a sad monotone. Our home seemed like a funeral home without the body of the dead person.

Once in a while there was a knock at the door, maybe a Girl Scout selling cookies. I watched with envy as Buelah opened the front door, put on her "public" smile, and made the purchase from the thankful Girl Scout. The little girl had no idea my wife was in deep mourning, so the conversation was light and easy. Then, as my wife shut the door and turned to face me, she once again put on the sad face that matched the feelings in her heart.

There were times when I wanted to grab her by the shoulders and scream, "Why don't you give me some of the smiles you've just given the Girl Scout?" I wanted so badly for her to put away the sad face that reflected the pain I didn't want to face. Looking back, I realize that her approach was far healthier than what I was doing. She was doing the hard work of mourning her loss.

Along my grief journey I have met countless men who, like me, have tried to outrun their pain by replacing it with something else. Whenever I see this happening, I remind them of an oil filter commercial. In that commercial a mechanic holds up a dirty oil filter and says, "You will either pay me now or pay me later." For grievers, the message is clear: if we try to stifle, ignore, outrun our sadness, and not talk about the pain we feel inside, there will be serious consequences down the road.

Guys especially try to "suck it up" and be strong. We've been taught since childhood that big boys don't cry. We take on the role of fixing it for everybody else when our own hearts are breaking. Facing my grief and pain is the toughest thing I've ever tried to do. On one occasion when my wife and I had just finished sitting through a support group, I walked to the back of the room to look over the books and pamphlets, materials designed to help bereaved couples. In front of me was a special pamphlet for men. I picked it up and looked carefully and could barely comprehend what I was reading. It was an instructional pamphlet giving step-by-step instructions to men, teaching them how to cry.

I opened it and read more. The author seemed to understand the ways in which grief can move from your heart to your throat, begging to be released. My eyes moved quickly to the words of instructions in which men were encouraged, if they felt their emotions coming to the surface, to look toward the sun or a bright light and to start panting like a dog on a hot August day. I was amused when I read this and instinctively knew there would not be a comparable brochure for women. Women already understand how to do this very well. We men are the ones who need to be coached. By the way, I've tried this method, and it works!

When I read the gospel account of the resurrection of Jesus, I see this pattern being played out there as well. It was the women who first made their way to the tomb as they mourned the death of Jesus. The disciples were together, talking about moving on to the next thing on their agenda—replacing. I tell men—and sometimes women—that the best way to get over grief is to *go through it*. If only it were that easy!

As Buelah and I tried to deal with the horror of losing Denny, it seemed to me we were in some sort of grief dance with each other. In our current cultural phenomenon of reality television is a show that's quite popular: "Dancing with the Stars." It's basically a dance contest, but it's unusual in that an amateur is paired with a professional dancer, and they're given several weeks to practice. Then they compete in a contest before judges and the entire television viewing audience. It's amazing to see just how much an amateur can improve when he or she is paired with an expert.

However, in our case, both Buelah and I were amateurs, and we were stepping all over each other's feet. Whenever she was in the pit of grief, I took the opposite attitude and tried to cheer her up by taking her out to eat or giving her flowers and gifts. I would do almost anything to try to lift her out of her despair. After several weeks of trying to cheer her up, I would become discouraged as I realized that we were going to be in this sad dance for a long, long time.

My personal journal reveals several times when I had questions about the survival of our marriage:

4/18/91

I wonder how long Buelah can go on like this. All I can do is hold her and let her cry. I'm so fearful her health will break. I must put my own grieving on hold and try to be strong for her, but it hurts so much. I wonder if we'll make it.

She also kept a journal, and her entry reveals the feelings she was having as we were stumbling along together:

7/22/91

I am extremely depressed. How can I feel any other way? Dennis has his work; he doesn't need me. No one needs me. It would be easier to die than to go on feeling this way.

How do people survive? I don't even want to. Why have you forsaken us? I have a right to be depressed. Sometimes I wish people would just leave me alone.

We had no idea we would be in this mode for years. The dance of grief was the hardest for us to learn. We had a strong desire to be with each other whenever we could, but when we were together it was always the same as before. I couldn't do anything right, nor could she. Across the coming months my anger continued to build toward her as you can see from the following entry:

4/22/92

Today began by taking Buelah to coffee before going to the office. She seemed happy, but before the day was over, she turned back to her depression and tears once again. At lunch time she began that old sighing again, and I asked her what that was for. She retaliated and wanted me to take her home because she felt I didn't want to be with her. She was right—I do hate being around her when she is that way. She has a neat way of looking and acting nice for others, but then she dumps all of her crap on me. This really makes me angry, and so today I gave her the silent (depression) act right back. I want her to get a little taste of what I get a whole lot of.

I can only imagine what it's going to be like when Andy leaves home. I find myself thinking about separating from her. I would never think of divorcing her, but I sure don't like living like this. I get about three good days a month. She won't get counseling, won't go to the doctor, won't develop any friendships—she just dumps it all on me. Tonight I'm really angry about this day and what she has done. It's almost like she can turn it on and off at will. Oh, God—I miss Denny so much. Why, oh, why must I go through this hell?

These hard feelings continued between the two of us. I wanted so badly to fix her and would make what I thought were helpful suggestions to her. However, it only angered her more and complicated her grief further, as you can see from her November 17 entry:

11/17/92

The pain continues. I don't feel like Dennis loves me anymore. I've lost him too. I've lost everyone and everything. Life will never be happy again. Dennis likes to criticize me. Lord, I know I deserve it.

After a while, I was sucked into that same pit and was ready to throw in the towel. Then, when she saw my despair, she would dry her tears and take on the role of trying to cheer me up. On rare occasions I allowed myself to grieve with her as you can see from the entry on 4/30/91. I was ending the semester as an adjunct professor and giving final exams at a nearby university, the same university Denny was attending at the time of his death.

It is so hard for me to see the death of a dream. Today at 1:00 P.M. I started my students on their final exams, and while they were taking the exam, I walked to my car, picked up Denny's books, and walked to the bookstore to return them. As I walked along with a heavy heart, I thought that Denny should be in one of those classrooms, taking his final exam, but instead here I am, his dad, taking his books, his science books, back to the bookstore to be returned for cash, $134.75. It was so hard to return them and acknowledge to my-self the death of a dream, the death of my son.

Buelah was grieving hard today, and I didn't plan

to tell her about my heaviness over the books. However, after supper I broke down and told her. I cried while she held me, and she was crying too. Later she said my sharing and grieving had actually helped her. Sometimes it's hard to figure women out. Maybe misery really does love company.

Most of the time it seemed as if we were on a teeter-totter. When she was down, I was up; when I was down, she was up. To be honest, there were times when I was so far down I wanted to simply slide off and let her crash without my counterbalance. I was that angry with her!

To be fair, I must also tell of the other losses she was experiencing. The year of 1991 was a horrible year for me but even worse for her. In February we lost Denny. In July our only remaining child, Andy, left us to spend six months in France as an exchange student. In August, the very next month, Buelah's mother had a severe stroke that nearly took her life. Looking back, we can point to that stroke as the time when Buelah truly lost her mother. After her stroke, Bea was barely able to function. Each time Buelah called her on the phone, I noticed her mom could only answer yes or no. There was no quality of life, and Buelah was forced to take over many of her business affairs. In those days, my wife was fighting to keep her own sanity.

Meanwhile, our home was a very sad place. We were mourning the loss of our son, worried sick about the other one, and also trying to decide how to help her mother, who lived 500 miles away. These were the worst days of our lives. A few people have asked if either of us took medication to help us cope with our losses. We chose not to take antidepressants. However, I know medication is sometimes necessary and always encourage people to follow the advice of their doctors in making that decision.

As I read through my journal entries while preparing to write about our experiences, I was surprised by the number of times I was distressed over Buelah's mood. I've tried to analyze my response to her and have come to somewhat of an understanding of myself.

First, when I looked at her sad face, it was as though I was looking into Denny's grave all over again. Her countenance reminded me of our loss, and I simply didn't want to face it in the same way she was handling it. Again, women mourn; men replace. We were good examples of this difference between women and men.

Second, something needs to be said that I've only recently learned and didn't know at the time: As a parent mourns the death of his or her child, the mourning *itself* provides the connection between the parent and child. My wife could not stop her deep mourning any more than she could have abandoned Denny when he was a little two-year-old boy in a crowded shopping mall. In other words, her grief was the invisible umbilical cord that kept the two of them connected. To her, to cut the cord would be abandoning him. As I read back through my journal 15 years later, I was astounded to see I was doing something similar. My grief was poured out in my journal, and I was surprised when I came across this entry:

5/17/95

Sometimes I wonder why I continue to journal. So much of this seems the same, much like my life is going these days, but I put my words down because it is one thing I attach to Denny's death.

Few grievers understand this truth, and it is the reason we become resentful of those who try to hurry us through our grief. To us who grieve, it feels as though they—the buck-up-and-get-over-it people—are trying to separate us from our child. We all know how dangerous it can be to come between a mother bear and her cub. Such was the attitude of Buelah when someone tried to take away her grief. To her, it felt as if they were trying to take Denny away. I felt the same way, too, but honestly it was stronger for her.

As we approached Christmas 1996, I noticed a change in myself as well as my wife. Unbeknown to me, she was coming to the place where she was making a conscious decision about her grief journey. Would she continue on in the same way she had been mourning over the previous years, or would she make a decision to try to go on and make the best of her life and the life of her family? She chose to lay aside the garment of grief and mourning, sweep up the ashes that surrounded her, and go on. It was November 1995, not quite five years since Denny's death. It was a turning point for both of us.

Across these years, I have encountered several men who have tried to fast-forward the mother of the dead child through her grief and suffering. If I can be of any help to another man about this, I would say that as hard as it may be, please allow her to express herself through her grief without being hurried. It may be the most difficult task you have ever faced, but stay with her and allow her to drain this cup of sorrow. She suffered through the labor pains as she gave birth to the child, and now she will likewise need your support as she faces the labor pains of grieving over her dead child. Don't leave the labor and delivery room too soon, or you may miss out when she delivers something brand new! By the way, I have noticed this same grief from adoptive mothers and dads who have lost a child. The pain appears to be the same.

Here is yet another observation I've noticed in blended families who have lost a child. The stepparent may have been very close to the child who died, but he or she is left out when it comes to experiencing the horrible grief when that child dies. There seems to be a private room called "grief and suffering," a room reserved for only the biological parents of the child. The stepparent may resent being left out of the inner circle where the "fellowship of suffering" is.

Since the death of our son, we have been in touch with many other bereaved parents who have made the decision to divorce. The thoughts of divorce also went through our minds, but we made a conscious decision to stay with one another no matter how dark and desperate things became. In the midst of heavy grief, it's easy to believe it when others tell you the divorce rate for bereaved couples is 70, 80, or even 90 percent. However, recent surveys reveal the opposite. A 1999 study by two University of Montana professors reveals that of the 306 people surveyed, only 57, or 18.6 percent, were no longer married. Of that 57, eight were widowed, yielding a divorce rate of 16 percent. This survey, combined with others, suggests a divorce rate of only 12 percent, far below the rates cited by various professionals (Mark Hardt and Dannette Caroll, "Bereaved Parents and Divorce," *Bereavement,* September/October 1999).

Sixteen years after Denny's death, we still have sore toes from stepping on each other's feet. A casual observer could easily look at us today and think we're both accomplished dancers as we move together as one.

It wasn't always that way. The truth is, we simply chose to stay with each other regardless of what happened. Each of us mourned differently and understood there were times we could help one another. Other times, we simply couldn't. It's called *commitment*. And while the death of a child was not mentioned in the wedding ceremony, the "for better, for worse" phrase caught it all.

My wife has never been more beautiful than she is now, and I can hardly wait to be in her presence. I'm so glad we held onto each other, even though we stepped on each other's toes. I'm glad we're still together, and we plan to continue this dance until they turn out the lights and send us home.

THREE

AM I LOSING MY MIND?

3/14/91

It seems I can visualize Denny so much better than I ever did before. I can close my eyes and see him perfectly—in his blue jeans and leather jacket, his hair always cut short and perfectly combed. It's almost like having his ghost in the house. If I didn't already know this was normal, I'd think I was losing it.

6/28/91

Buelah, Andy, and I had pizza at Godfather's, one of Denny's favorite pizza places. I looked at Denny's empty chair and could almost see his ghost eating pizza with us. I noticed when the three of us had had our fill, we still had pizza left, about the same amount Denny would have eaten. These days, when we go out for pizza, we usually take some home. It wasn't that way when Den was alive.

10/28/94

This evening a young man came out of the church and walked past me. I particularly noticed his head— the shape of his head. The color and length of his hair were very much like Denny's. I watched a long time as he walked away. Could it be that I need to grieve more? The dreams I had last night, the boy I noticed, may be signals that I need to talk about my pain more. I don't know.

I was standing in the check-out line at the hospital dining room when I noticed him: a fresh-looking young intern wearing a white coat with a stethoscope around his neck. As I stood behind him, I noticed several things that reminded me of our son: his height, the shape of his head, the color of his hair. For a few brief moments, I was tempted to believe this was indeed our son standing in front of me, getting ready to pay for his lunch. Denny had already announced his intention to become a medical doctor, and for a brief moment I found myself hoping I had had amnesia and was just now coming back to my senses. As I looked again at the back of his head, my mind was begging me to believe that the trauma of my loss had been an illusion and that our son was actually alive.

Psychologists and grief counselors understand this phenomenon and try to help patients realize that there's a period when the bereaved person thinks he or she has seen the ghost of the person who died. Grievers usually do not realize how deeply their thinking processes have been affected by their loss.

Soon after Denny died, I realized I was in deep shock but didn't want to believe he was indeed gone from us. The ritual of the visitation and funeral helped me accept the fact this was no dream and that he really was dead. These days I see an increasing number of people who choose not to go through the ritual of a funeral or memorial service. Later they wonder why they need the help of a psychologist or therapist.

In the days and weeks following the funeral, I began to realize this devastating loss had affected me more deeply than I first imagined. It was as though lightning had struck my brain, leaving charred pieces everywhere. My mind and thinking processes were very different. My short-term memory was almost nonexistent. For example, prior to his death I could look at a phone number and then quickly dial it without looking back at the number twice. After Denny died, I caught myself looking back three or four times at a telephone number before I could finally dial it.

At church, I looked at the faces of people I had known for years but could not recall their names. I found ways around addressing the person. Sometimes with guys

I would say, "Hey, buddy," or with ladies I called attention to their dress or the colors they had chosen to wear to church that day. I found a way to compensate for my lack of memory and desperately hoped people would not notice the fact that I could not remember their names. Inwardly, I was worried and wondered if I was in the early stages of Alzheimer's disease.

Perhaps the best way to explain this phenomenon is to compare it to the memory capacity of a computer. Think of the difference between RAM and ROM. RAM is random access memory, while ROM is read-only memory. When buying a computer, it's important you have plenty of random access memory so you can store hundreds of megabytes of memory for future access. If a particular software program takes up too much RAM, the computer may slow down considerably or not function at the expected speed.

Similarly, when a person suffers a traumatic and shocking loss such as the death of a child, the brain is on overload as it tries to process the loss. I had trouble remembering telephone numbers, people's names, what I was supposed to pick up at the grocery store. I missed appointments at the office, and my secretary soon realized I needed to be reminded several times through notes and verbal reminders. During counseling sessions I got people's stories and histories confused and had to apologize for not remembering details they had told me previously. My brain had a virus called grief, and I felt as if most of the files had been deleted.

Soon after Denny died, I was completely absorbed in my loss no matter what I was doing. My mind was on him and his death all the time. It was pinned to the front of my mind. While driving home, I would forget to take my exit and suddenly come to my senses several miles down the interstate. Or I would be so caught up in my thoughts about Denny that I would catch myself driving considerably over the speed limit, unaware that I was speeding. Nothing else in life seemed to matter, and I was amazed the rest of the world hadn't come to a stop. I wanted the whole world to stop, sit down, and grieve with me and my family about this overwhelming loss. Everywhere I looked, I saw signs of death and heard sounds of mourning. Late at night when I couldn't sleep, I could hear in the distance the mournful sound of a train whistle as it called our entire city to mourn his death.

As I look back, what surprises me most is the length of time I was in this forgetful mode. I was not alarmed during the first few weeks when I realized that my circuits were on overload. However, when this condition extended into months and even years, I secretly wondered if there was something very wrong with my mind. I kept this fear to myself and told no one, not even my wife. I was holding onto my sanity by a thread and trying hard not to let anyone else know how afraid I was. I identified so much with C. S. Lewis, who, after losing his wife, said, "No one told me that grief felt so much like fear."

There were times when I tried to trick myself into believing Denny was still at the university he had previously attended in Illinois. This trick seemed to give my mind a break from the awful pain and provided a way for me to bear it. As I started to come out of the shock of what happened, I was afraid I would lose my mind. It's hard to explain to others just how fragile one feels at a time like this. It's hard to tell what's normal and what's abnormal.

Across the years I've heard many stories of how people could use their minds to disassociate themselves from the reality of what was happening, such as physical or sexual abuse. For example, women and men alike have told me that they could imagine themselves to be hiding under the edge of a heating vent or in the ceiling while the abuse was happening. Somehow they could use their minds to escape the horror of the situation. I understand better how that works since I've also used this technique a thousand times, trying not to feel the pain of our loss.

My journal entry of 2/16/91 indicates the method I was using in order to cope with the staggering pain:

It's almost as though there's a box deep within my emotions. Every once in a while I can remove the lid—just a little. When I do, I see Denny inside, dead. I quickly put the lid back on and go on my way, because I can't possibly stand the pain.

I was making a strong effort to keep Denny's death in a box and forget it ever happened. The problem with this method is evident. When I tried to forget his death, I forgot a lot of other things along with it.

People often ask me how I was able to overcome my forgetfulness. I answer by sharing a number of things that have helped me.

- First of all, lighten up. Refuse to take yourself too seriously.
- Realize this condition is temporary and that in time your memory will kick back in. It will pass.
- In the meantime, write down what's important to your everyday functioning.

Technology allows us to keep our contacts, appointments, and lists on handheld devices. I've thanked God over these years that the Blackberry arrived just in time for me.

Along with the loss of memory came sleepless nights. Looking back in my journal, I noticed this entry:

3/14/91

Last night after I finished journaling, I could not get to sleep. I called my brother Joe in San Diego and talked a long time. Then, I still couldn't sleep and went down to the kitchen and talked with my brother Scott until 1:30 A.M. Still, I couldn't sleep very well. I hope this isn't the signal of a deep problem. Previous to this I have been able to sleep fairly well.

While I was experiencing these sleepless nights and loss of memory, I noticed that my wife was rapidly losing weight and had no appetite. On 3/15/91 I wrote the following in my journal:

Buelah continues to mourn a lot. Her appetite is still nonexistent. She eats only because she knows she should. I don't know how to help. I take her out to eat, usually twice a day, out to shops and stores, anything to get her mind on something else. We each had such a wonderful relationship with Denny, yet it was different. She is so wounded. I miss her laugh, her smile. I see only sadness and tears now. I wish I could make her laugh.

Even though our friends brought in enough food to

feed an army, neither my wife nor I had much appetite. I could not persuade her to eat much, and I watched helplessly as she continued to lose weight. She lost nearly 40 pounds and two dress sizes. She grew weaker and thinner. Normally she cried herself to sleep, and I often tried in vain to comfort her. Then, on the night of 4/8/91 something unusual happened:

Something very strange happened with Buelah tonight in bed about five minutes ago as I was journaling. She started panting, and as I turned my head to look at her, I saw that her eyes were open but not focused—like what I have seen on the face of a dead person before. I spoke her name, and she finally came out from under the "spell" she was having. She told me she could not help herself and was unaware she had been panting. I asked if she had been dreaming, but she wasn't sure. This all seems so strange, and I hope she's OK.

Other entries in my journal show that on occasion she would call me to return home quickly because she was having a panic attack. I was struggling to keep my own sanity and trying to help her at the same time.

The entire family seemed to be experiencing the effects of grief at the same time. Our son Andy had made plans to travel to France as an exchange student prior to

Denny's death. When the exchange organization heard about Andy's brother's death, they were very concerned about his grief and not sure if he should continue with his plans to be an exchange student in Europe. The idea of his leaving home, traveling to a foreign country, and spending several months with a family we had never met seemed out of the question to us. We had already lost one son, so our tendency was to be overprotective with Andy. We discussed this for several days. However, we finally came to the place at which we were able to fight off our fears and sign the permission papers. I remember thinking, *Denny died right under our noses here in our family room. I really have no control over anything.*

Prior to Denny's death, I had no clue about the many ways a parent is affected by this kind of loss. I remember seeing the sad faces of other bereaved parents in our community but had no idea of the mental and physical pain brought on by the death of their child. The consequences of this type of death are often hidden from the casual onlooker.

Not long after Denny died, I was experiencing panic attacks myself. At my wife's urging, I visited our family doctor for a checkup. I noticed the frown on the doctor's face when he read my EKG and realized something was wrong. He wanted another test, and I was soon taking a brisk walk on a treadmill with several electrodes attached to my chest. I failed the test and was sent to a cardiologist. After an echocardiogram, the cardiologist, who was a member of our church and aware of our son's death, came into the room where my wife and I waited. He read the results of my exam and seemed to intuitively know the reason for the change in my heart rhythm.

I'll never forget that moment when he looked at me with tears in his eyes and said, "You'll need to take special care of yourself. Please get some exercise and lose a few pounds." I nodded to him, indicating that I would try, but as we left his office I began to understand more fully how a person can literally die from a broken heart.

Since Denny's death, I've observed several people who died only a few months after the death of their spouse. For example, Johnny Cash's death certificate listed "complications from diabetes" as the cause of death, but his fans are aware of the fact that he passed away just a few months after June's death. Mimi Guameri writes in her book *The Heart Speaks*, "Doctors will tell you, broken heart syndrome or stress-induced heart failure is a medical condition—and a perfect example of the heart's power and vulnerability." She goes on to say "This condition seems to be caused by high levels of hormones that the body produces during severe stress, which can be temporarily toxic to the heart." In other words, you can die from a broken heart, and these days medical science is able to observe this happening in grievers. Now when I see people in deep grief holding their chests, I realize just how vulnerable they really are. Sometimes I felt as though I would die too.

I took the doctor's words seriously and tried to force myself to get more exercise, but my heart wasn't in it. I had no will to go with the plan the doctor had laid before me. Later I found out why.

When a person experiences the trauma of losing a child, it affects his or her body chemistry in a deep and profound way. Our hormones regulate our state of mind as they are produced by special organs and tissues in our bodies. Hormones notify the body of changes outside and inside the body that must be responded to in order to maintain health. For example, if the mind interprets a situation as threatening or frightening, regardless of whether the danger is real or imagined, adrenalin and several other hormones are released into the blood that make the body alert and ready for action. Likewise, when a person experiences the loss of someone close, the body is flooded with a sudden outpouring of stress hormones from the sympathetic nervous system. As one study shows, after a major loss, such as the death of a spouse or child, up to one third of the people most directly affected will suffer detrimental effects on their physical or mental health or both.

Such bereavements increase the risk of death from heart disease and suicide as well as causing or contributing to a variety of psychosomatic and psychiatric disorders. About one quarter of widows and widowers will experience clinical depression and anxiety during the first year of bereavement. The risk drops to about 17 percent by the end of the first year and continues to decline thereafter. Clegg found that 31 percent of the 71 patients admitted to a psychiatric unit for the elderly had recently been bereaved (<<http://findarticles.com/p/articles/mi_m0999/is_n7134_v316/ai_20440212>>).

There's a mind-body connection we must acknowledge as we deal with grief issues. Our joy, creativity, and contentment can all lead to a state of mind-body harmony. Likewise, fear, anxiety, stress, grief, and depression all contribute to mind-body disharmony, which increases risks for a variety of illnesses. Most physicians understand this connection and encourage their bereaved patients to get adequate nourishment, rest, and exercise.

Across the years I've noticed the growing number of persons who, like me, had a major illness or hospitalization not many weeks or months after someone close to them died. I've had two telephone conversations just today with grieving persons who are suffering with severe emotional issues that require the help of a mental health professional. When I mentioned the death of their loved one, they seemed surprised by my suggestion and had a hard time connecting the dots.

On the very day we took my mother-in-law, Bea, back to the airport, Buelah and I were keenly aware that we were going back to an empty house for the first time since Denny's death. We had to face the empty house, the place where he died, by ourselves. Although I didn't write about it in my journal, I vividly remember pulling our car into the garage. The engine was still running as I turned to Buelah and said, "All I have to do is reach up to the visor and press the garage door button and we can lean back in our car seats, hold hands, close our eyes, and die together."

She looked at me and smiled weakly. "Yes," she said, "I know it's very tempting. But we could never do that to Andy. But—if we didn't have him . . ." She didn't finish her sentence, but we both knew how tempting and easy it would be to slip out of our pain. We both wanted to die and felt it would have been a wonderful gift if somehow we had a legitimate way to leave this world.

This feeling continued for nearly five years. We were not seriously suicidal, but we had no desire to live either. It's hard to admit, but it's a feeling shared by countless bereaved parents. I know, because they share these thoughts with me time and time again.

I can't end this chapter without bringing up the

topic of dreams. It was Buelah who had the first dream of Denny just three nights after he died.

3/9/91

> *Last night Buelah had her first dream about Denny. He told her he was OK and very happy. Buelah didn't want to tell me, not wanting to make me feel bad. She also said he still had his big, beautiful smile. I wonder when he'll appear in my dreams too.*

Several months later I began to dream of Denny. However, my dreams were not as pleasant as Buelah's.

10/13/91

> *This day began in a traumatic way—with a dream. Last night I dreamed I was in a chapel, and two caskets were there. Denny was in one, and someone else, an older, baldheaded man, was in the other. Both caskets were lined up on the left side of the sanctuary. It was a sanctuary similar to the Word of Life Chapel in New York. It had quite a steep grade, sloping toward the front. I was walking past Denny's casket when I saw his eyes open just a little. He was lying on his stomach or back, but his head was turned sideways, toward me. Anyway, he opened his eyes, just a little,*

and I first thought it was just some kind of nervous reflex. But then he fully opened his eyes. I'll never forget the vivid, alive look of his eyes as he raised up, smiled, and sat on the edge of the casket with his legs dangling over the side. I rushed up to him, threw my arms around him, and he put his arms around me and held me for a moment.

Then I awoke. It was over—only a dream—and I was in a cold sweat, awake at 4:45 A.M. It depresses me, and today was so hard. Somehow the dream seemed to make me more aware of Denny today, and thoughts of him were so very strong. My grief seems almost double now. I just wonder if the full weight of my loss is really beginning to hit me now.

It doesn't take a rocket scientist to see that my dreams were calling me back to do the hard work of mourning my terrible loss. What I was unwilling to face in my conscious hours, the dreams expressed in my sleep. Across these years I have come to respect my dreams and the messages I need to take from them. This is yet another thing I have learned. There's a very strong mind-body connection, and the pain we're experiencing will somehow express itself through our dreams or even our bodies.

By the way, the person in the other coffin in my dream was my beloved grandfather, and I came to realize this a few nights after my dream. Grandpa Apple was the very first person I loved and lost by death.

FOUR

WHERE IS GOD?

4/2/91

Tonight Buelah asked the question that's been bothering me for a long time: Does prayer really matter? Does God care about losses like this? Is He punishing us for something? I'm not sure of anything anymore. I simply don't care! The most precious thing has been taken away from me, and I want to say to God, "OK—you win! Whatever you want, go ahead and take it. I don't have the heart to care any more. There's nothing left—go ahead and shoot me, too, if that's what you want. You could have stopped this, but you didn't. You let our precious son die, and here we are, empty-handed and broken."

If you go back and check the weather report for ZIP code 66062 on February 6, 1991, you'll find that it was an extremely foggy morning. I noticed the dense, gray fog when I first awakened. I had no idea the fog would become symbolic of the deep spiritual fog I would soon enter.

The night before Denny died, Buelah and I knelt by the place where he was resting, laid our hands on his head, and prayed earnestly for his healing. As a pastor, I had done this countless times for people in hospitals, nursing homes, and in my office at the church. Since childhood, I had believed that prayer changes things and had listened to countless people witness to the answers they received in response to prayer.

I had always trusted in the words of Jesus found in Scripture: "I tell you, whatever you ask for in prayer, believe that you have received it, and it will be yours" (Mark 11:24). However, on February 6, 1991, everything I believed about prayer was challenged when God did not respond to my most desperate prayer.

As I recall the events of that morning, I noticed the thick fog and could barely see the neighbor's house as I looked out our bedroom window. I prepared a bowl of cereal and then checked on Denny. It was at that moment when I discovered he was not conscious, not breathing, and it wasn't long until, as described earlier, it was obvious that he was gone. In that tragic moment I felt as though God had abandoned me, and I identified with Jesus' words when He screamed out from the Cross, "My God, my God, why have you forsaken me?" (Matt. 27:46). I would scream out those words several times in the days to come as the fog enveloped me and my family.

I would never have said this out loud to anyone, but in my mind I had the mistaken idea that tragedies like this simply don't happen to those of us who are ministers. I'm not quite sure where this notion came from, but I suppose it has something to do with the Old Testament story of the first Passover as found in Exodus 11-12. The children of Israel gained protection from the death angel as they placed the blood of the Passover lamb over their doors as instructed by Moses. The firstborn of all Egyptian families were slain on that fateful night, but the faithful Israelite families were safe. I thought we were safe too! Looking back, I have told others that I had the "Passover mentality" but realize now that being a minister does not exempt me from tragedy.

After serving nearly 40 years as a pastor, I've observed the different reactions of people just after they have experienced unexpected trauma in their lives. Some are drawn closer to God, and their faith is renewed as they move to a deeper level in their relationship with Him. On the other hand, there are just as many, if not more, who feel as though God has let them down when they needed help the most. Their cry, like mine, is "Why have you forsaken me?"

My disillusion about the care and protection from

God is very apparent as you read through my journal, especially the entry on March 9, 1991. It had been exactly one month since we had buried our son, so I made my way out to the cemetery alone. I stopped the car and walked the few feet to his grave. As I approached, I noticed a new grave. Someone else had been buried at the foot of Denny's grave, and I immediately noticed that it was Rhoda's grave.

Rhoda was a sweet senior adult who died just days after Denny, but no one from the church office had notified me of her death. Perhaps they knew she was buried at my son's feet, and they had compassion on me and kept her death from me. I knew her story and had been making pastoral calls on her for several weeks prior to her death. Years earlier she had been involved in a serious auto accident and, as a result, had to be given a blood transfusion in order to save her life. In those days there was only limited knowledge about HIV, and the screening procedures were very primitive compared to today. Many years after her accident, she was called by the Red Cross and asked to come in to their office so she could be tested for HIV. The results of the test revealed she had been given blood tainted by HIV. Over the years I visited her and watched as she grew weaker.

I walked around both graves and thought about the unfairness of it all.

3/9/91

I stood by both graves, raised my fist in the air, and said, "Oh, God, you've got some explaining to do about this!"

I was angry, confused, and doubted that God cared much about the innocent victims of these senseless tragedies and mistakes. I was still in shock, trying to understand all that had happened.

Perhaps this is a good place to talk about shock and what it felt like for me. I believe shock is a merciful thing God does for us when we experience the loss of someone we love. I compare it to the Novocain a dentist injects into a patient's gum in preparation for treatment. The dentist is careful to numb the area so the patient feels no pain while the dentist does his or her work—usually with a drill.

God protects us by placing us in deep shock when we experience tragedy. The length of time this shock lingers will vary from person to person, depending upon the circumstances of the death and the relationship with the deceased person. The "soul-numbing" effect of shock allows us to somehow make it through the planning of the funeral as well as the visitation and funeral ritual itself. Quite often the onlookers will observe the lack of emotion of a person in shock and exclaim, "Did you notice how well he [she] is doing? I didn't see him [her] crying at all!" Little do they know that the survivors are in a deep, soul-numbing state and are not able to feel the full effects of their loss—yet.

Looking through my journal, I noticed it was between six and eight weeks when the shock began to wane and the full force of our loss began to hit us. My wife and I were still in a daze. We were trying to understand what had happened to us, trying to make sense of this overwhelming nightmare. As you can see from the journal entry above, it was almost one month after Denny's death when she looked at me through her tears and asked the question I also had been asking myself: "Does prayer really matter?" We would struggle with that question for several years.

In those early days, I was having a difficult time concentrating, but I found myself reaching for books such as Philip Yancey's *Disappointment with God* and Harold Kushner's *When Bad Things Happen to Good People*. I wanted desperately to know why this had happened. At the same time, I struggled in my attempts to read the Bible and finally came to discover that I, too, was disappointed and angry with God.

This became obvious whenever I heard someone talking about their guardian angels. Beliefs I had previously held about God were now coming up for a vote once again. On several occasions I could barely contain my anger as I heard others discuss how they narrowly escaped being killed in an accident because their "guardian angels" were watching over and protecting them. I tried my best to join them in their good fortune, but inwardly I was thinking, *Where was my son's guardian angel on the night of February 6?* I was disgusted by their naive assumptions. I wanted to tell them that guardian angels were in the same category as Santa Claus and the Easter bunny.

As a pastor, I found myself in a spiritual dilemma. How could I continue my duties as pastor, trying to help others, when deep down I was strongly offended and feeling let down by a God who had seemingly ignored us in our time of deepest need? At first I decided to keep this spiritual dilemma a secret. I made my way through each day by performing the duties that were expected of me, visiting those in hospitals and nursing centers, counseling troubled persons in my office, performing funerals and weddings. In short, I was trying to minister to others but also attempting to deal with the question my wife had posed to me about whether or not prayer really matters.

I held that question in my mind as I journeyed through those months—even years. Looking back, I call this my time of desert wanderings, and I've noticed that many other grievers go through this as well. To my way of thinking at the time, God had walked away from me, and I felt like an abandoned child. Dust formed on my Bible, and my faith was at an all-time low. I prayed only when it was expected of me, and I often walked out of hospital rooms after praying for the sick, wondering if God truly had an interest in the well-being of the person I had just prayed for or if this was simply a waste of everyone's time.

I've told others that at that time I felt like an offended child who had just quarreled with his father and announced he was leaving home. However, after packing the suitcase and opening the back door to leave, the child suddenly realizes he has no place to go.

I felt as though I was hanging out near the back door of my faith. Everything felt dull, dead, lifeless. While others seemed to enjoy life in high-definition color, mine was like the steady rain on a gray tombstone at midnight. I had no direction, no ambition, and I didn't care. Once in a while someone would ask me what I was experiencing and what it was like to grieve so hard. I thought about it and tried to come up with adjectives that could help describe this horror to them. I tried telling them, but there were no words to describe this sort of tragedy. The best I could compare it to was to say that it might be as if I were an astronaut on a spacewalk all alone while others were safe in the mother ship. When an astronaut goes for a space walk, he or she is always tethered to the mother ship by a cord that supplies the oxygen and electrical power needed for the tasks and well-being of the astronaut. I felt as though I was on a spacewalk and found myself without the umbilical cord connecting me to the mother ship. I was floating aimlessly in space. This continued for years, and I felt as though God was gone from me forever.

The words of Job after he had lost everything seemed true for me: "If I go to the east, he is not there; if I go to the west, I do not find him. When he is at work in the north, I do not see him; when he turns to the south, I catch no glimpse of him" (Job 23:8-9). I was alone with my questions. I didn't know that God was doing severe work on my soul while I was still in the fog.

In the spring of 1993, just two years into my grief journey, I was still struggling and simply trying to exist. The local hospital was offering a special hospice training course for ministers and chaplains, and I decided to take advantage of this training. It was a huge mistake. I sat and listened to stories of people dying and how to help them in their final days, and I left the training with more anxiety than I had before, but I didn't know what to do with these feelings.

I returned to my office and tried to help out with the

upcoming Easter pageant. It was a large production that required the work of more than 500 people. Every staff member was expected to help, and I had taken on the job of coordinating the shuttle bus drivers as well as the traffic directors, all of whom worked outside the church sanctuary. It was simply too much for me to go into the sanctuary and watch the scenes portraying the death of God's Son. When I heard the music and watched the drama, all I could think about was the death of my own son, so I chose to work outdoors and stay clear of those reminders.

On this particular day, April 7, 1993, I needed to talk with a university student who was helping me coordinate the workers outside. When I called and tried to reach him, I was told he was in choir practice and that the choir was practicing in the main sanctuary. I was told he would be available at the conclusion of choir practice at 1:30 P.M. I waited until 1:15 and made my way over to the sanctuary with a very heavy heart. I walked in through a back door and sat in the shadows, under the balcony. The choir was assembled off to the side, and neither the choir nor the director had noticed my slipping in one of the back doors to hear them finish up. The front of the church looked like something from the set of Universal Studios. Artists had been at work for several weeks, assembling huge decorative screens and sets in order to give the appropriate background and tell the story of the last week of Christ's life. I sat there alone in the darkness, wondering if it was all a farce!

I thought the choir had come to the end of its practice, and a quick look at my watch told me it was time for practice to conclude. However, the director had said to the choir, "I know we're about out of time, but I want you to go over one more song before we dismiss." I didn't pay much attention to the song he had selected and was impatient that he was holding the students beyond the allotted time. As I fidgeted in my seat and wished he would hurry, the pianist played a strong introduction. Then I heard the first notes of the choir as they nearly shouted, "Fear not, for I have redeemed you!"

These opening words shot across the sanctuary like an F-16 fighter jet making a low pass. The atmosphere suddenly changed. I knew immediately that God had placed me in this location for a special reason, and in a sanctuary that seated almost 4,000, I sat alone as a congregation of one. God had my full attention. I knew from years of Bible study that when God wants to say something important, He always begins with "fear not." The lyrics were taken from Isaiah 43:

> Fear not, for I have redeemed you; I have summoned you by name; you are mine. When you pass through the waters, I will be with you; when you

pass through the rivers, they will not sweep over you. When you walk through the fire, you will not be burned; the flames will not set you ablaze. For I am the LORD, your God. . . . You are precious and honored in my sight, and . . . I love you. . . . Do not be afraid, for I am with you *(w. 1-5)*.

When they finished singing, there was a holy hush in the sanctuary, and I was almost afraid to breathe. God had just spoken to me, and I felt as if I should remove my shoes—I was on holy ground.

I sat for several minutes, holding my white handkerchief to my eyes, wiping away the tears. Things were different now. Until this moment I had felt abandoned by God—alone in a fog of grief and suffering. Through this choir and His own words, God had revealed His love and concern for me. I felt Him saying to me, *I know where you are and what you're going through. I want you to know that I love you and that I am with you.* God was with me! The knowledge that God was with me made all the difference in the world! David, in Ps. 23, wrote it and I had read it a thousand times: "for you are with me" (v. 4). I now had a personal confirmation at a time when I needed it most. God was indeed with me.

This life-changing experience reminded me of the experience Isaiah had with God at a pivotal moment in his life. Isaiah experienced the presence of God in the midst of his grief after King Uzziah died. I had preached a number of sermons from this passage, but since Denny's death I now see it in a different light.

Isaiah had entered the Temple at a very low time in his life. The opening words of Isa. 6:1 speak to me: "In the year that King Uzziah died, I saw the LORD, seated on a throne." It is believed the prophet Isaiah was a cousin to King Uzziah, so the untimely death of the king caused Isaiah to experience a deep sense of loss. When the Lord appeared to the prophet, everything changed, and it was in effect a time of commissioning for Isaiah. God asked, "Whom shall I send? And who shall go for us?" Isaiah obediently responded by saying, "Here am I. Send me" (v. 8).

This experience, while not on the same level as Isaiah's experience, was something of a call for me, and my ministry began to take a new turn. People were approaching me for guidance and counsel. In the days ahead I became more open about my doubts and questions, about my internal pain and homesickness for my son. As I shared this pain with others in the church, a new ministry opened to me. As one of my colleagues said to me one day, "Dennis, I believe God is using you to teach our church how to grieve."

This holy experience was taking me in a new spiritual direction. However, I still had the questions about prayer in my mind: "Does God really care about our prayers? Does prayer really make a difference?" I pondered this for several more months and tried to gain more understanding. Gradually, I came to the place in which I accepted the fact that we live in a fallen world, a place where the rain falls on the just and the unjust. In the midst of my spiritual dilemma about prayer, I came to a crossroads and asked myself two questions: *Do I believe there's a sovereign God who knows and sees all, including my suffering over the loss of our son? Am I going to trust in this sovereign God whom I don't always understand?* I pondered these questions for a long time and finally came to the place in which I said through my tears, "Yes, I believe in Him, and yes, I will trust Him."

These days, when I pray for something or someone, I'm trying to follow the teachings and example of our Savior, Jesus. I follow His instructions in Matt. 7:7 to ask, seek, and knock. However, I'm keenly aware He prayed earnestly, even three times, for the cup of suffering to be removed. Eventually He came to a place, as we all must, where He bowed at the altar of God's will: "Yet not my will, but yours be done" (Luke 22:42).

After my Isa. 43 experience with God in the sanctuary, gradually the questions I had asked previously didn't seem so important any more. Our great God had noticed my pain, my suffering, and used a choir to communicate this wonderful truth to me. I was not alone! I still felt as though I was in the dense fog, but I knew I was not alone any longer.

Driving a car in the fog can be tricky, and there are a few things you need to remember. First, drive slowly and keep your headlights on low beam. Another trick I've learned is to pay attention to the white line on the right side of the road. That line is a reference point that will keep me on the road and in the correct lane.

When it comes to the fog of grief, the rules are similar: go slowly and give yourself plenty of time. Keep your eyes trained on the lines that have served you well in the past. It may seem as though God has forsaken you, but He is still there with you, even though the fog may hide Him for a while.

FIVE

I DON'T WANT HIM
TO BE FORGOTTEN

11/20/93

Buelah and I had coffee and then went to the store. At noon I went to the Hestons' home and took pictures of their family together in front of their fireplace for their Christmas card. As I looked through my view-finder at Ron with his two sons and grandsons, I felt so cheated. I wish so much I still had Denny and would someday have his children too.

It was an ordinary Sunday afternoon until the phone rang. The senior pastor of our church asked if I would take his place as chaplain and join the Kansas State Highway Patrol as they faced the hard task of making a death notice. I quickly dressed, drove to headquarters, and met the state troopers. We formed our plan and made our way to the home, where we would inform an unsuspecting wife and mother that her husband and young son had died instantly in an auto accident. In addition, we would share the news that her remaining son, also in the accident, had been rushed to a nearby trauma hospital where emergency surgery was already underway.

When she opened the door and saw the uniformed officers, she knew something was terribly wrong. Her husband was more than two hours late getting home, and she had seen the breaking news on television that showed a picture of a wrecked car that looked similar to the one her husband drove. As she opened the door and saw us, she screamed and said, "Oh, my God—it really *was* them!"

We went inside and made the sad announcement of the two deaths. I watched as she went into shock, then quickly made her way down the hallway to her daughter's bedroom. We waited in the living room as she told her daughter what had happened. Their home became a place of unbelievable horror as the mother and daughter held each other and screamed out their agony.

I tried to comfort them as best I could and after several minutes took them in my car to the hospital, where the surviving son was in surgery, fighting for his life. In the emergency room we were given the tattered clothes of the son, who was in surgery. She took the clothes, and we went into a private room where she could be away from the growing number of reporters who were trying to get an exclusive for the evening news.

We had been sitting in the hospital waiting room

for several minutes when the bereaved wife and mother turned to me and said, "Pastor, today I've lost both my husband and son. Can you tell me why I'm grieving more for my son than for my husband?" It was one of those moments of awful truth when she expressed her honest, unedited feelings.

I don't recall my answer, and I'm sure it was not adequate. However, after losing a child myself, I now have a better understanding of her feelings and why she would be so concerned about grieving over her child more than her husband. It has to do with the loss of our legacy, along with the natural maternal instincts to care for her children.

I've heard it said, "When I buried my parents, I buried my past; when I buried my spouse, I buried my present; but when I buried my child, I buried my future." In the privacy of my office, I have had several widowed people who also lost a child confess to me that they grieved the loss of their child more than the loss of their spouse. My wife and I together have led several grief groups at our church and have noticed the unique pain of those who have lost a child by death.

Losing a child is in a class by itself. I suppose we all desire to live a good, long life. We expect to see our children grow up, get their educations, marry, and have their families. We look forward to seeing our children's children so we can enjoy the role of loving grandparents, take them to Disney World, carry their pictures with us, show them off, and brag.

The death of a child creates a domino effect. I can easily point to several other losses that came to us as a result of our son's death: future birthday celebrations, graduation ceremonies, wedding showers, wedding, first real job, baby showers, birth of a grandchild, celebrating holidays, new house celebrations, and the celebration of job promotions, just to name a few. The list of things we have grieved includes the loss of our dreams. The journal entry of 4/26/92 reveals that the loss of dreams was uppermost in my mind:

> *I went to early prayer meeting at 7:00 A.M, then over to McDonald's for a roll and coffee. I took the roll and coffee to Buelah, and she was awake after a bad night. She dreamed about Denny when he was a baby. She's had three or four of those since his death. As I got ready for church this morning, I went downstairs, turned on some music, and looked at our family picture a while. Then I looked at Denny in his picture. It's still so very hard to do that. I looked at the fireplace and the hearth where I sat and held Denny's head while he slept by the fire. Then I looked at the ashes in the*

fireplace and thought of how the ashes so represent my life and dreams. Denny's death has changed everything for me.

I believe God has formed us in such a way that we want to leave something of ourselves behind after we're gone. We want to be significant—to feel we left the world a better place than when we found it. There's an ingrained drive within us to have children, plant trees, and write books. All of these are what we leave behind us when we die.

I recall standing by his open casket in the funeral home and looking at his face. He not only had my name but he had my chin, the same color hair, my nose, my eyes. He carried my DNA, and in him was much of my future. When he died, I didn't lose just him—I lost all that he carried of me in this world.

After the death of our son, I recall another funeral of a young man who also happened to be friends with my son. He was a great-looking kid and had lots of friends. The girls were crazy about him, and he had no problem finding dates. He died in a tragic accident, and I vividly recall a conversation we had with his mother beside his casket during the visitation. She knew we had also lost a child, so there was an instant connection between us. I recall that she looked both ways to make sure no one was listening. Then she whispered to us, "I know I shouldn't think this way, but I'm just hoping a little pregnant girl will show up tonight, telling me she's pregnant with my son's baby." Looking back, I understand why she felt that way. She was hoping to keep her legacy alive. It's a very real concern for parents—to keep the family tree branching out.

In the beginning of our grief journey, all we could think about was the loss of our son. In the months and years that followed his death, we cringed when we received invitations to wedding showers and weddings. We began to understand the ripple effect this loss was going to have on our lives for several years to come. My wife has shared with me the times she forced herself to go to wedding showers, only to excuse herself so she could find a private place to cry.

Grieving parents keep a mental record of the age of their child, and they carefully watch those who were friends of their child as they continue on. We notice when our child's friends get married and when they come to church with new babies. At first it was so painful that we dreaded going to church and seeing the new babies. We tried to protect ourselves by not walking past the church nursery. However, there have been times when we could not avoid seeing the children of our son's friends. For example, I recall sitting on the platform at church on a particular Mother's Day when Denny's former girlfriend came forward to the altar with her husband and newborn baby. I watched with envy as the parents and grandparents dedicated their baby to God. I was wondering what the baby would have looked like if Denny had been the father of the child. These are the things that run through grieving parents' minds when they consider the loss of their legacy.

I'm the oldest of ten children, and most of my brothers and sisters are grandparents. They all know of my strong desire to be a grandparent, and they often keep their grandparent stories and pictures away from us, because they feel it will cause us more pain. However, I'm glad for their good fortune, and these days I'm trying to be the best uncle I can possibly be to these wonderful children in our extended family. My wife and I are coming to the place where we are increasingly able to enjoy other people's children and are trying to be substitute grandparents to them. While we still grieve not having our own grandchildren to love, we can care for and love others as we leave behind a legacy of friendship and support to other children. God has graciously given us children in our local church fellowship who run into our arms each Sunday. I hope their grandparents understand how special these gifts from God are. It's their legacy.

In the beginning years of our grief journey, we felt cheated and cut off in this world. Today both my wife and I are trying to help bereaved parents by teaching them creative ways in which they can keep the memory of their child alive. The following are just a few of the things we're doing, plus other ideas parents have shared with us.

Scholarship Fund

Soon after our son died, a good friend whispered to me that it might be a good idea to create a scholarship fund for medical students. Instead of flowers, we gave people the option of contributing to a special fund we set up in his name at the nearby university. Each spring we try to be present as the special Denny Apple Medical Scholarship is awarded. We've kept in touch with some of the medical students who have received this award, and it's an encouragement to us to know that Denny is having a part in the lives of others who have gone into the field of medicine.

Commemorative T-Shirt

A few years after Denny died, I started running and entered several races. When I prepared myself to run the Chicago Marathon, I made sure to include Denny's picture and "1972-1991" on the back of that shirt. I had several runners tell me they had also lost a child and thanked me for wearing Denny's picture that day.

Greeting Cards

During the year we send out several birthday and anniversary cards to my parents, brothers, sisters, nephews, and nieces. When I sign these cards, I always sign: "Dennis, Buelah, Andy, and Denny," being sure to place a heart around Denny's name. We don't want him to be forgotten.

Jewelry

A few years ago I took both Denny's and Andy's photographs to a jeweler, who was able to use a special laser method to etch the pictures onto two small, gold, heart-shaped pieces. I had the dates placed on the back of Denny's heart, and my wife wears this piece of jewelry frequently. Whenever anyone comments on it, it gives her the opportunity to tell about our sons—both of them! Many funeral homes will be glad to take a print of the thumb and create a piece of jewelry that can be worn as a necklace or bracelet.

Trees and Flowers

Our son loved flowers and all things that grow outdoors. So it was especially appreciated when students from the nearby university planted a tree in his name on campus. We planted rose bushes in our yard that were given in his memory as well. When we see these flowers, we're reminded of him.

Legacy Web-site

At our church we've set up a special Web-site where pictures and stories can be posted, each one telling the story of someone we loved and lost. If you go to this site at <ccnlegacy.org> you will see those whom we are keeping alive through this wonderful technology available to us today. Go ahead and click on the "A-B" section, and you'll find our son Denny.

Today it's easier than ever to create a Web-site where you can post pictures and display some of the things your loved one created while he or she was alive. You can even show short video clips and share videos of your loved one talking, singing, or playing an instrument. This is a wonderful way to create an electronic scrapbook.

Candle-lighting Ceremonies.

The second Sunday in December, The Compassionate Friends conducts a special ceremony at 7:00 P.M. It's usually cold and sometimes snowy here in Kansas at that time of year. This is usually conducted in a nearby park, and I always make it a point to attend this simple but meaningful ceremony. Every bereaved parent is given a candle, the child's name is read, and the parent steps forward and lights the candle in memory of his or her child. I wouldn't miss it! It always warms my heart to hear Denny's name read.

Pictures

A few years ago a friend told me about an artist who took the separate photographs of her five grandchildren and made drawings of these same children all on one canvas. I thought it was a good idea and was impressed with the work of this particular artist. So I took the photographs of both our sons to him without my wife's knowledge. He was able to create a beautiful drawing of both sons on the same canvas. I had this piece framed and gave it to her on our wedding anniversary.

After a special dinner together, I gave her the box to unwrap so she could discover what I had given her. When she pulled out the framed picture of both our sons, she gasped and started crying. I cried along with her as we both admired the beautiful piece the artist had created for us. The picture of our sons is prominently displayed in our home and allows guests to bring up the subject of our sons, a subject we're always glad to talk about.

Commemorative Brick

The university where my wife and I met and received our higher education notified us that they were construct-ing a new building and would be placing commemorative bricks at the entrance. For a certain price we could have Denny's name and the dates of his life inscribed on one of these bricks. We jumped at the chance to do this, realizing that it would be one more way we could help keep his memory alive. Whenever we return to the campus, we always take time to visit the place where these memorial bricks are laid, and we remember him.

Church Rituals

At the church where I serve, we provide special times when grievers can remember their loved ones. For example, at Christmas and Easter, persons can memorialize their loved ones by purchasing either an Easter lily or poinsettia. The flowers are beautifully displayed at the front of the sanctuary during these special seasons of the year. Then, on the Sunday before Easter or Christmas, a special bulletin insert is printed with the names of the deceased loved ones as well as the names of the family members who made the donation. After the service, the family members can take the flower home and enjoy it.

Pulpit Flowers

Most Sunday mornings in front of the pulpit is a special bouquet of flowers donated by family members who wish to remember their loved one. We usually do this either on the date of Denny's birth or his death. Again, the family can take these flowers home after the service.

Christmas Night of Remembrance

The Christmas Night of Remembrance is a special

service, usually on a Sunday. Grievers meet in a smaller chapel and take some unhurried time to meditate about the life of their loved ones. The service is usually led by people who have lost someone during the last year. There are songs, Scripture readings, and prayer. The highlight of this night of remembrance comes when each person is invited to stand, say the name of the deceased person, and share one thing he or she will always remember about him or her. "Silent Night" is played softly in the background as the grievers stand to their feet and tell their stories. After the service, the grievers are given opportunity to take a luminary and place it on the sidewalk near the street by the church and are given a commemorative Christmas tree ornament with the name of their loved one and the date on it. Later, in the large sanctuary during candlelight Communion, there's special recognition at the end of that service for those who are grieving. After Communion has been served and before the benediction, someone will step forward and light a special candle of remembrance. The pastor then invites all persons who have lost someone by death to come forward while everyone sings "Silent Night." All the grievers stand together while the pastor prays the benediction.

Wedding Candle of Remembrance

I've conducted hundreds of weddings, and when either the bride or groom has a deceased sibling, I'm always glad to see a special candle of remembrance at the wedding ceremony honoring the one who has died. This simple act of acknowledgement is heartwarming to the parents. It doesn't cost much and will go a long way in helping the family deal with the missing face in the wedding party.

Memory Quilt

Our son was a tri-athlete, and we have several drawers full of T-shirts from the many events in which he participated. A few years ago, my sister-in-law Jean asked for the shirts so she could make a quilt, using a different T-shirt for each block. This quilt is very special for us, and we proudly show it off. Behind each T-shirt block is a story, and we're always glad to tell it.

Items for Your Car

It's common these days to see the RIP initials hand-painted on the back window of a car. They're usually accompanied by the deceased person's name and the dates of birth and death. This seems to be popular with younger drivers. However, you can also have your child's name and dates placed on license plate holders as well. Special decals can be made and placed on the back or side windows also. Just recently I conducted a funeral for a young man in our community who was an outstanding guitar player. Many of his friends now have decals that show a guitar and their friend's name, Jack. It's their favorite way of remembering him.

Donate a Book in the Person's Memory

School and church libraries are wonderful places to donate books in your child's name. The librarian will guide you in having your child's name placed in the front of the book you're donating.

Bronzing

Bronzing is a creative way to create a keepsake from your loved one's personal items. Recently in one of my support groups, a couple told me they planned to bronze the work shoes of their deceased son. He loved to work outside as a landscaper. The bronzed shoes will help keep his memory alive as they recall the times he tracked mud into the house after working on a special project in the backyard.

Plaster of Paris

Another way to remember your loved one is to have a plaster of Paris casting of your loved one's hand. Many funeral homes offer this as an option, and the detail in these pieces is astounding. Several parents have told me they're glad they did this.

Biography of Your Child

Take time to write a biography of your child, listing his or her accomplishments in school, sports, or any other activity he or she enjoyed. Be sure to include some of the humorous stories about your child. Capture these items before your memory fades and you're not as sharp with the details. It may be hard at first, but you'll be glad you completed it. When finished, make copies for friends and family. They'll thank you for it.

Keeping our children alive through these creative means will insure that they won't be forgotten. There are no better historians for our children's lives than us, their parents. Don't let your legacy fade away without telling and showing the world what a wonderful person your child was and how much he or she meant to you.

SIX

HIS BIRTHDAY
IS COMING . . .

3/1/94

*Today Denny would have celebrated his 22nd
birthday had he lived. You never forget your children's
birthdays. I recall that early-morning ride to St. James
Hospital in Chicago Heights, Illinois, the short amount
of time in labor, and Dr. Ianucci saying that Buelah
had done very well, "Not one hair out of place." She
looked as though she had just walked out of the salon.
And while I was not allowed to witness his birth, I recall the day the nurse placed him onto the bed in front
of me and said I could take him and Buelah home. I
was very close to Den . . . I watched over him, changed
him, fed and played with him, and was there for him at
every turn. For almost 19 years he brought us so much
happiness—our lives are so much richer for having had
him as our son.*

*But tonight I must confess to a deep longing I have
to feel his arms around me, to hear his voice, to share
jokes and funny stories with him. It still hurts, and I
know it does for Buelah too. Even as I write these lines,
she's lying beside me, crying. No, I did not witness his
birth, but I was the one who found him dead. How can
I ever forget?*

Birthdays are very big at our house. If you want
to know the birth or anniversary date of anyone in my
family—I am the oldest of ten—just ask my wife. She can
give it to you faster than your laptop can find it. She's
a "frequent buyer" at Hallmark card shops and will
sometimes spend hours searching for that perfect card
to send a friend or relative. I've lost track of all the times
she's approached me in the aisle of a card shop, holding
three or four cards in her hand, and asking me, "Which
one of these cards do you think will work best for him?"

If Denny had lived another 23 days, we would have
celebrated his 19th birthday. The house would have been
full of family and friends. The long dining room table
would have been set and decorated with bright napkins.
In the center would be a special birthday cake made by
our friend Marilyn. Brightly colored helium-filled balloons
would be tied to Denny's chair, and Buelah would have
made sure his favorite food was on the table. We would

have gathered around the happy table, and I would have been seated in my usual place at the end.

When it came time to eat, we all would have held hands, and I would have given thanks for the food, being sure to thank God for Denny's life and that he was born into our family. After the meal, Buelah would have brought out the custom-made birthday cake with the candles already lit. I would lead the group in singing "Happy Birthday to You" while we watched the light of the candles dancing in his happy eyes. There would have been cameras flashing as we tried to catch him blowing out 19 candles.

After he blew out the candles, his mother would have started cutting the cake, passing a piece out to everyone around the table, asking if they cared for ice cream, too. Before everyone could finish their birthday cake, it would have been time to open cards and birthday gifts. He would have opened the cards and packages while I took several pictures to record the event. It would have been a great party—but it never happened. Instead, our home felt like a dimly lit museum, filled with memories from the past.

I recall that first missed birthday. We had a hard day, and I noticed it was especially difficult for Buelah. At bedtime she was crying into her pillow, and I was ready to turn out the bedside lamp and welcome a deep sleep that would relieve my pain. I looked into her sad eyes and asked her a question: "Honey, if you had known 19 years ago that Denny would not live to see his 19th birthday, would you have wanted to give birth to him, raise him, only to lose him like this and experience this nightmare?"

She looked at me, and through her tears she said, "Oh, yes, a thousand times over. I would do it all over again."

I nodded in agreement, knowing I would have wanted the same. I turned out the light and held her in my arms as we went to sleep, remembering birthdays from the past.

The first missed birthday was a nightmare, and I had assumed it would be rough. What surprised me was how the future birthdays and holidays also affected me. I thought I was ready for the big ones, such as his death date, birth date, Christmas, and Thanksgiving. We tried to brace ourselves and prepare for those, but we were blindsided by all the other holidays when families gather together for cookouts and fun. Memorial Day, Independence Day, Labor Day, Father's Day, and Mother's Day are also family gathering times. It was very painful when we tried to do something special together. I remember forcing ourselves to enjoy a cookout on July 4, but I recall thinking, *When we're all together, we still aren't all together.*

Denny's empty chair seemed emptier than usual on those special family days and holiday weekends. I found myself wishing we could somehow skip these family times and simply stick to a yearly calendar without holidays.

In those early years, we soon found ways to help us deal with the calendar pain. For example, the first Christmas we faced was without either Denny or Andy. Andy was still in France as an exchange student and would not be returning home until January, so we postponed our family Christmas celebration until his return.

When Buelah and I made our way back to Indiana to be with family, we simply could not face the idea of going to Mom and Dad's and watching my younger brothers and sisters with their children. Instead, we made reservations at a hotel near the airport and stayed away from the rest of the family on Christmas Eve. We did join them the next day for the traditional Christmas party together, but we found a way to escape some of the pain of Christmas Eve. Somehow, it helped us and made the first Christmas more tolerable.

No one told us about—nor were we ready for—the sneak attacks that would come after we lost our son. By sneak attacks I mean those things that seemed to pop up when we were least expecting them. For example, my journal reveals certain days when I was bombarded with thoughts of Denny everywhere I turned.

4/27/91

Today has been a difficult day for me because of the memories of Denny. Everywhere I look I see things that remind me of him. This weather has been picture-perfect, and I think of how much Denny would enjoy it. I saw a young boy mowing a lawn; a dad teaching his son to drive a car, complete with jerky starts and stops; Scott, my brother, riding Denny's bike. All these things—and more—remind me of him.

These are the things that happen to us most anywhere, anytime. Still, there were several more that I was unprepared for. My journal entry of 8/28/91 reveals the day I was sitting in my office and working when there was a knock on the door and a university student by the name of April appeared and said she wanted to talk to me:

She walked into my office and presented me with a yearbook. I noticed the engraving on the front: "The Apple Family." I immediately suspicioned something and asked if Denny's picture was in it. She nodded and told me where to look. Sure enough, toward the back was a full page dedicated to Denny. His picture, along with President Spindle's tribute, was there. Rosa, my secretary, and April watched as I melted in a moment of deep

emotion. I whispered, "Thank you," and clutched the
book to my chest and cried. They both slipped out of the
room and left me to my thoughts and tears.

There were several of these sneak attacks that came
from everywhere. I recall sitting in the weekly staff meeting with the other ministers on our staff. Our youth
pastor, Ron, was rejoicing one morning that he and his
wife, Sharon, had just heard the first heartbeat of their
very first child, Katie Rose.

5/3/91

This morning, Ron Jackson, our youth pastor, told
us he heard his baby's heartbeat for the first time. I
immediately thought of Denny and wished to God that
I had heard his heart beating on the morning of Feb. 6.

Other times, I might be riding in the car and would
see something that reminded me of him.

10/29/94

I had a sneak attack on the way to the play. I saw
a large, grassy lawn in front of an insurance build-
ing and was reminded of Denny because of the way
he mowed a lawn. Den knew how to make a lawn look
nice. As I looked over the lawn, I was surprised at the

pain I was feeling, but no one else in the car knew how much I was hurt.

Some of the worst sneak attacks came when some of the other young people in our church died. On the weekend of June 26-28, 1992, we were in Nashville for a special weekend of orientation for new students. Andy would be starting school there in the fall, and we were there with him. We drove back on Saturday night. On Sunday morning we received a phone call from another staff pastor, a call that would rip our "grief scab" open once again.

6/28/92

Our day began with a phone call around 6:30 A.M. from Paul Fitzgerald, telling me that Robbie Jones, one of Denny's friends, had been killed in an auto accident late Friday night, and that Kendra Seaman, who was also riding in the car, was critically injured. I could scarcely believe it! I told Buelah, and we both cried. Later I went to Sunday School and church, encouraging Buelah and Andy to stay home. Everyone was watching me throughout the morning, asking if this whole thing was bothering me. It was!

Weddings were hard for me but much harder for Buelah. She often stayed home and didn't attend most of them. There were a few we simply had to face and force ourselves to attend, even though the pain was horrible. One of these times was the wedding of Denny's best friend, Greg. The entry from 2/27/93 tells what happened that day.

I walked down the hallway earlier in the day at church and saw the young man who would be in Greg Sheffer's wedding. All of a sudden I could see Denny. Since Greg and Den were best friends, I knew Den would have been his best man. I later begged Buelah to not go, because I didn't want to go to the wedding either. However, we went late, sat in the back, and endured the ceremony. I couldn't bear to look at the front of the church, for I knew Denny was not there. It was devastating for us both. We left quickly at the end and rushed up to the reception hall, and I signed the guest book. Just as I finished, they both walked in. I turned and congratulated them and walked out. It was all I could do. Later, we drove to Denny's grave and cried while his friends celebrated at the wedding reception. Sometimes I really wonder if God cares about us.

Another thing that surprised me in those early years was the dread of the upcoming calendar dates. At first it was the dread of the sixth day of each month. March 6 was especially painful. My journal entry from March 4 reflects the painful flashbacks I was having as I tried to brace myself.

It is hard to believe, but we are almost to the one-month anniversary. I know exactly what I was doing one month ago today. I took Denny to the doctor in the morning, then to Wal-Mart to get the medicine. I remember having him sit in the little snack-concession area and drink a soft drink while I had the prescription filled. I remember how I nearly ran to him with the medication I thought would help him. Instead, I was rushing to him with the medication that would help kill him. I just didn't know. That night I had a fire in the fireplace and tried to help keep him warm. I remember holding his head by the fire for a long time. Little did I know at that moment it would be the last time I would hold him. He thanked me for holding him after he awakened. Later, Buelah and I kneeled by his bedside and prayed for him. We knew he was so very sick, but little did we know that would be the last prayer for our sick boy. Yes, I remember one month ago very, very well.

Gradually, the sixth day of each month would become more tolerable for me, but February 6—at 8:20 A.M.—is still an annual time of pain. It is the 9/11 of my life, and that date is seared into my mind and emotions.

Each year as we approached our annual appointment with pain on the calendar, I noticed a deeper-than-usual depression would sweep over me. For example, as we finished with Christmas and New Year's, I tried to prepare myself for the next two hurdles: February 6 and March 1, his birthday. No matter how hard I tried, I could not keep myself from falling into a deep sadness and lethargy. In the days leading up to these painful dates, I recall sitting in staff meetings, never saying a word, feeling invisible to everyone in the room. The dread of the date was almost as bad as the date itself. Then, when the date was past, I would feel as though I had made it over another hurdle and would feel somewhat relieved. The whole year seemed like a long-distance steeple chase in which I was constantly trying to jump over barriers and deep-water pits.

These sneak attacks surprise us through any of our five senses. We may be pushing our cart through the grocery store and see his favorite box of cereal on the shelf. We may even reach for the box and start to put it into the cart, only to painfully remember that no one eats that brand of cereal at our house anymore. We may be walking through a department store and catch the scent of his favorite cologne. All of a sudden our minds race back to the last time we hugged and kissed his neck and enjoyed that pleasant fragrance as he hugged us.

Sometimes these grief attacks come in places we would not suspect, such as an elevator that plays background music as you move between floors in a large building. The music may mean nothing to others standing beside you, but you remember this as the tune he always sang in the shower when he thought no one could hear him. That tune used to make us smile; now it breaks our hearts.

You may be puzzled by the strong thoughts of your loved one every time you eat chocolate ice cream. Then you remember later that it was his favorite flavor, and the two of you had such wonderful conversations over heaping bowls of it.

Every time a young man squares off and playfully hits me on the shoulder, I'm instantly taken back to the days when Denny tested his strength against mine by hitting me on the shoulder.

Sometimes we're very aware of the effect of these sneak attacks. Other times we're not aware of the sensory experiences we associate with our loved one. However, these reminders are still registered in our brains, and we may find ourselves feeling irritable and even angry later on and not be in touch with the reason.

When these reminders seize upon us, we can quickly be reduced to tears. Sometimes we can control these feelings by steering around these known places, such as the scene of the accident. Other times something is suddenly in our minds, and we can't avoid it no matter how hard we try.

When someone new comes to our grief support group, I gently remind him or her that we're going to "lean into the pain," and the box of tissue on the table reinforces the direction we'll be moving during the weeks of the support group. The members of the group understand this and realize they need to face their pain.

This is quite different from the moments when we're blindsided by a memory or event. This is one of the great benefits of a support group. One of the tasks of the facilitator is to gently lead the group members back through their painful memories so they can tell the story about their personal loss. At first it seems overwhelming and frightening to step into their painful stories once again. Their fears can make them feel like small children going into a haunted house alone on Halloween night. But when grievers know that others in the group will walk through their haunted story with them and stay close, it doesn't seem quite so frightening.

My wife and I recently took a small group of bereaved parents through an exercise that caused them to revisit their pain. Our method of doing this was simple. We brought a pile of old magazines and placed them on the table before them. Then we gave each person a large poster board and asked each to turn through the magazines, looking for either pictures or words that reminded them of their dead child. They were instructed to cut out the pictures and words and then paste them onto their individual posters. We encouraged them to fill the entire poster. My wife and I joined them, and we worked for several minutes together. All you could hear in the room was the sound of scissors and of pages being ripped out of the old magazines.

When we had finished this exercise, I held my poster up for all to see, and then pointed to each picture and told them why it reminded me of Denny. In turn, each person followed suit, and we were able to cry and laugh together as we shared the stories of our children. It was an unforgettable night.

One particular story was unusually funny. I noticed one of the mothers cutting out a picture of an old antique typewriter. She carefully pasted it onto the poster board. When it was her turn to share the stories associated with the pictures on her poster, she told about her son's wit and humor. He was always thinking of funny and unusual things to do, things that didn't cost much money. She told about the day he decided to remove an antique typewriter from their storage room so that he could take it to Starbucks. This son had noticed how Starbucks seemed to be filled with people working on their laptops while drinking their espresso. He thought it might be fun to haul in this old typewriter and place it on the table and hammer out a few pages while drinking his coffee too. She told how he took great delight in typing a few lines and returning the carriage just after the loud ding of the bell. Obviously, he enjoyed the stares and laughter this caused as he mocked the hardworking Starbucks customers.

All of us in the support group laughed with his mother as she told of this incident in the life of her son. We'll never forget it, and it helped her to "lean into the pain" as she told this story to us. Support groups are wonderful places where we can stay close together as we tell our stories to one another. They're an important part of our recovery. I believe we can lessen or diminish the sneak attacks as we learn to face these painful reminders together.

This idea of leaning into the pain is not new. In fact, you'll find it in the Bible. Take a look at Jesus and how He restored Peter. Notice how it so resembles what we do in our support groups. Prior to His trial and death,

Jesus told Peter that before the rooster crowed twice the next morning, he would deny Jesus three times. Peter exclaimed that although everyone else might deny Jesus, he himself would never do so. Later that same night, Jesus' words about Peter denying Him three times came true, and the Scriptures record how he went out, called curses upon his head, and wept bitterly (Mark 14:72.) In this story it's important to note where Peter was standing and what he was doing when he denied Jesus. He was standing by a fire, a charcoal fire, trying to warm himself. This was a traumatic moment for Peter, a memory he would wish to erase from his mind but could not. Jesus knew about these painful memories, and the last chapter of the Gospel of John tells the record of the way in which Jesus restored Peter.

In the last chapter of John you'll notice that Jesus called Peter from the boat where he had been fishing to join Him for a breakfast of bread and fish. In this dialogue with Peter you can't miss the connection between the three earlier denials and the three questions Jesus placed before Peter: "Do you love me?" When Jesus asked Peter these three questions, it was as though He were taking him back to that awful night, the one Peter had been trying to forget—the night he turned on Jesus and denied Him.

But there's more to this story than first meets the

eye. As they were having this conversation, the smoke from the fire was curling up and into the nostrils of Peter. It was the smoke from a charcoal fire. The original Greek language reveals only two places in the New Testament in which a charcoal fire is mentioned. One is in the courtyard where Peter denied Jesus. The other is at this point on the seashore. Jesus knew exactly what He was doing when He chose to use charcoal instead of the driftwood along the shoreline to build the fire that morning. Jesus, the master therapist, worked with Peter in such a way that He gives us a wonderful example of doing therapy with a person who needed help in his recovery.

I've thought about this passage several times and how it relates to grief and sneak attacks. I can only imagine what Peter's life might have been like if Jesus had not restored him in the way He did. If this restorative therapy had not been done on Peter, there's no doubt he would have cringed every time he heard a rooster crow. Or he would have been reduced to tears every time he warmed himself beside a charcoal fire. In short, he would have had these awful reminders of his pain, of his failure.

Jesus, knowing all these things, gently took Peter back to the scene of the crime as He asked the question three times while Peter smelled the painful smoke. John says nothing about a rooster crowing, but it would not surprise me if the distant crowing of a rooster could be heard during that early-morning breakfast dialogue.

Jesus no doubt knew that in the future Peter would still be rattled whenever he saw the number three or heard a rooster crowing twice. He would still wince when he smelled charcoal burning. But right behind those painful reminders would come the memory of Jesus' restorative words of confidence when He commissioned Peter to "feed my sheep." This is a great biblical example of "going through it" in order to help a person "get over it."

When a griever has one or several of these painful grief attacks crashing into his or her mind and emotions, it causes a pressure to build up, not unlike the steam pressure that builds up in a pressure cooker. When this happens, it's important to find someone to whom you can confide about your internal pain. When someone chooses to be your companion and truly listen to your pain—without trying to fix you—you can begin to find relief and decrease the internal pressure.

If I were in the bumper-sticker business, I would highly recommend this one for grievers: "Sorrow Shared Is Sorrow Halved." When we have someone—or a group—to acknowledge our pain, we'll walk away from the conversation much lighter, taking on new courage to face the future.

On one particular occasion someone helped me in a special way. It was on a Sunday night, and I was sitting in my usual place at church on the platform between two other staff members. That night we had a missionary speaker from the Amazon jungle. He was also a physician and told stories about his work as a missionary doctor.

He told a story about a family with a small baby who had contracted a fever and died. The father and mother of the dead child quickly rushed the baby to a canoe and made their way down the river to the doctor's home. The missionary went on to tell how the mother screamed when she came up the river bank with the dead baby in her arms.

To dramatize his story and make it seem more real, this missionary doctor planned for his wife to come through one of the back doors of the sanctuary, complete in native dress and holding a toy doll. She entered the sanctuary, playing the part of the grief-stricken mother. As she threw back her head and came out with a gut-wrenching scream, the whole crowd was suddenly startled. We had no forewarning that this was going to happen, and I instantly recognized that scream. It's seldom heard, but when you hear it you know the worst has happened.

When I heard that scream, I instantly stiffened and

wanted to leave my chair on the platform and run out of the room. It was one of those sneak attacks, and I had nowhere to go. Suddenly, I felt a hand on my arm, and it was my friend Bill, sitting next to me.

It's hard to describe what his touch meant in that moment, but it was a touch that acknowledged my pain and said, "I know this is hurting you, and I'm right here with you. We can go through this together."

I made it. And so can you—with help.

SEVEN

I LOVE MY CHURCH—BUT SOMETIMES IT HURTS TO BE THERE

6/2/91

Today just seemed hard for me. I thought about Denny so much. People try to encourage me. The visiting minister who spoke tonight told me he understood how I feel. But I had a notion to look him in the eye and say, "You have absolutely no idea of how I feel." Right now I feel as though a bomb has gone off in my emotions and everything has been blown to bits. I can't put it back together; I don't know where to begin. Oh, God—please help me to begin, with even tiny steps, walking toward you again. I have no one else to turn to. You must help us!

When our Denny died, the first ones to arrive in our home were the people from the church—my ministerial colleagues and those who were in our small group of close friends. Our dear friends Terry and Ethel even took leave of their missionary work in Arizona and drove all night so they could move in and help us through our most trying days. Our close friends in the church were the ones who came in to handle the phone calls, answer the door, arrange for meals, and make sure we were cared for. They formed a cocoon of care around us 24-7. Each knock at the door brought food, flowers, and kind words of support along with promises to pray for us.

I don't know what we would have done without the warm, loving support from our church. While many have given up on the institutional church, I would be the first to say we could never have made it without their support.

A few days after the funeral, we were in Denny's bedroom and were gently looking through his personal belongings. At this point, his room seemed like a sacred shrine, and we were reluctant to change or move anything that was special to him. In his closet I noticed a blue, plastic, portable file, so I took it out and carefully opened it. Inside was a collection of short essays he had written while he was a student at Olivet Nazarene University. I lay on the floor of his bedroom and read through every essay, savoring each word like a starving man enjoying a gourmet meal. My journal entry on February 12 records this discovery.

As I looked through the many pages, I was especially drawn toward an essay entitled "Apathy Toward the Church Hurts the Family." In this paper, which he had written about two months before his death, he spoke of how a happy church produces a happy family and vice-versa. He also said, "If a loved one is lost (died), the church will help comfort the family in their time of loss." Denny said many other wonderful things about the church, but I was especially drawn to a special sentence he had written: "This world is not a good place to be left alone in." How true! Denny had come to see and understand the real value of his immediate family and his church family. He had no way of knowing when he penned these words that the church would comfort and carry us as we mourned his death. He would be very pleased to see how our church is loving us. Somehow I think he knows all about it.

Looking back, I can see where the prayers and love of our church carried us when we could not help ourselves. I can't imagine our trying to endure this nightmare of losing our son without them. Denny's funeral service was held in the church sanctuary, and we'll never forget the outpouring of love as the people came to stand and suffer with us in our darkest hours. We can

never repay them for opening their hearts and support-
ing us, not only in those immediate days following his
death but also through all these years since his death.

Still to this day, people who knew Denny will come
up to us and share stories about him. It always warms
our hearts when someone takes the time to share a
memory about him.

Our church was a place of support, but it was also
a place where we were misunderstood and wounded as
well. My journal reveals February 24, 1991, as the date I
returned to my usual place on the platform.

*Today I sat on the platform for the first time since
Denny's death. I found myself looking toward the
section of seats where the teens and college students
usually sit. Sure enough, one was missing! Somehow
I hoped I would see the big smile on a boy handsome
enough to be a model with his arm around a beautiful
dark-haired girl.*

Grieving in front of thousands of worshipers is not
easy. I recall the first Sunday I returned to the platform
and how frightened I felt when it came time to walk
out and take my seat. Our morning worship services
had about 2,500 people in attendance, and although I
had been serving as a staff minister four years, this first

morning back after our son's death felt as if it was my very first day and produced the anxiety and apprehensions you feel when you're new. I felt awkward, unsteady, and was glad I didn't have any significant part in leading the worship service that day.

I could feel the eyes of sympathy on me as I settled into my customary chair on the platform. My platform chair was large and made of solid oak with high arm rests. It felt safe, but over the next few weeks I wished for a seatbelt to hold me in place as I endured the "hurry up and get over it" messages.

Normally Buelah would be with me in both the morning and evening services at church. After Denny died, she could manage to attend only the morning worship hour. She usually sat back under the balcony so that her crying would not disrupt the worshipers nearby. Sometimes someone would sit with her and try to give comfort, but still it was hard for her to be in church. After the worship service was over and everyone walked out the door, she would see complete families walking out together, and it was a painful reminder of what she would never have again. For her, going to church with me was expected, and she did it in order to support me as one of the pastors.

Soon after Denny's death, our church had an emphasis on spiritual renewal and had a visiting speaker.

My journal entries reveal that there were no fewer than four messages based on the scripture found in Rom. 8:28 within the two weeks after I returned to church. The death of our son had, no doubt, hit our congregation like a terrorist attack. The result was that families were wondering, *If one of our pastors was not spared, could this happen to us as well?* So the messages to the worshipers were filled with admonitions to trust in the sovereignty of God, shake off the past, and move on, keeping in mind that all things work together for good and that this—our son's death—would ultimately be for the good.

I recall one message in particular from a visiting minister who titled his sermon "When There Are No Answers or Action from God." He obviously understood that the church was in shock, so he tried to fix the situation with his message.

Over the next few months we had several guest ministers speaking on topics designed to help fast-forward our church through this dark time of grief. Behind the platform and prior to the services, there would be moments of uneasiness as visiting ministers prepared to speak to our congregation. However, as we stood next to one another in the back corridor before the start time of the worship service, they never said anything to me or acknowledged the death of our son. They chose instead to do their counseling from the pulpit. I found myself wishing and hoping someone would simply ask how I was holding up during my personal nightmare. If anything was said to me, it was usually to ask how my wife was doing, ignoring the pain I was experiencing.

I'm not quite sure what was going on in the minds of our church members when it came to the subjects of death and grief, especially grief from an "out of order" death like our son's. Perhaps they had bought into the idea that believers, and especially ministers, have the hope of heaven and seeing our loved ones again. Therefore, we had no need to grieve our loss. Or perhaps they thought about the words of Paul in 1 Thess. 4:13: "Brothers, we do not want you to be ignorant about those who fall asleep, or to grieve like the rest of men, who have no hope."

Quite often I hear Christians use this scripture to infer that because we have the confidence and hope of heaven, we should not grieve like the rest of the world. While it's true that we grieve differently, this scripture does not teach Christians to smile and bravely face our losses. It simply reminds us of the difference between our grief and the grief of those who have no hope. There certainly is a difference, but Christians are not emotionless robots. If Jesus cried over the death of His friend Lazarus, we certainly have the right to cry over the death of our loved ones too.

Inside our altars, at the front of the sanctuary, is a hidden shelf where we have several boxes of tissues. We keep them there because of the heavy sorrow people often bring to the altar when they pray. Tears are the messengers of grief, and I'm amazed by how many grief issues are brought to the altar of prayer each week. This grief is often accompanied by much emotion and many tears.

Years ago I heard our altars referred to as the "mourners' bench." I've not heard that reference in a long time, but we still have a lot of mourning happening at our altars. The mourners' bench is a place where people can kneel to pray, expressing their remorse and grief over their sinfulness and separation from God. Whenever I see a person crying at the altars at the front of the church, I will not step in and try to hush them from expressing their soul pain. I believe it's healthful for them to drain their cup of sorrow, because at the end of their mourning will come a new person—a new faith.

In much the same way, a person who's grieving the loss of someone in his or her life must be given space and time to grieve. We dare not try to rush this process. It takes as long as it takes.

In those early days of my grief journey, I had several minister friends, as well as members of the church, who seemed very uncomfortable with my grief and sadness. Looking back, I'm quite certain it was an awful experience for them to be around me or my wife. It seemed to us they often used scriptures to try and cheer us up. One scripture in particular that was used in order to cheer us up and move us away from our sadness was 1 Thess. 5:16-18: "Be joyful always; pray continually; give thanks in all circumstances, for this is God's will for you in Christ Jesus."

They would tell us to be joyful and give thanks for Denny's death and to praise God in all circumstances. Some of my minister friends told me, "Christians with a strong faith will come through this faster."

I listened to them and secretly wished they would finish what they had to say and move on—out of my presence. The people who said these things were never people who had lost children. Those who had lost a child knew better.

There were others here who were a bit more subtle in their attempts to cheer us up. For example, barely six weeks after our son died, folks would greet me with a big smile and say, "Good morning, Pastor. How are you doing today?" When I heard this sort of greeting, I wanted to spin around and say, "I am doing about as well as you would be doing if you had lost your child six weeks ago." Only God knows how many times I thought those words; thankfully, I never said them out loud.

Across the years, I've noticed the ways in which people in the church react and respond to other members who have lost a loved one by death. Almost always will come a predictable set of questions that will be asked of the grievers: "How old was he or she?" "Did he or she know the Lord?" It seems to me there is a subtle inference behind these two questions, and it goes like this: "If your loved one was a Christian or if he [she] lived to a ripe old age, then you shouldn't feel so sad about your loss. After all, you'll see him [her] again in heaven." It's as though these people are the grief police, not wanting us to express our feelings of sadness. They want us to buck up and get over it.

The music at church can feel very unfriendly for grievers—especially for a grieving pastor. I love to sing the songs of faith and can lead the worship music when called upon. The death of our son changed everything, and the songs seemed different and out of place for me. For example, when the worship leader asked us to stand and sing the praise chorus "God Is Good All the Time," I found the words sticking in my throat. I could not honestly sing what I didn't believe. After a few attempts, I stopped the singing and simply stood on the platform with a sad face and a heavy heart. Inside, I was feeling betrayed by a God I thought loved me at one time. I could not be congruent with my feelings by singing such happy praise songs.

The midweek prayer services could also be a time of deep wounding. A few months after our son's death, there was a terrible car crash near the church that resulted in the death of one of our outstanding teenagers. Sitting next to him in the car were two other young people. One escaped with minor injuries, but the other one had severe head trauma and was hospitalized for several months. We all prayed fervently for her as she went through several more months of rehabilitation.

Then, one Wednesday night, she was able to return to church for a midweek prayer service. Another one of our pastors was leading the prayer time, and when he saw her come into the chapel, he called her by name, asking her to come to the front so that everyone could see the "miracle" God had performed.

As I watched her walk to the front of the chapel, I saw the tears on the face of the mother whose son died in that same accident. My heart broke for her as she watched this survivor give thanks to God for sparing her life. How much better it would have been if we could have taken time to also acknowledge the loss this precious mother had suffered as well. To me, the greater miracle was found in the fact that she was in church, even though she hadn't received her miracle. Her prayer had not been answered, yet she was still trusting God.

Since my son's death, I've talked with several other

bereaved parents who expressed the same thoughts about their churches. One man told me that since his child's death, he has transferred to a church that offers more of a formal liturgy for him to follow during the time of worship. I asked his reason for doing this. "In my old church, they told me how I was supposed to feel. In this new church, I can simply go and worship as we move through the liturgy before us. They don't expect anything from me—they simply let me be there, even with my grief. All they do is hug me."

Going back to church, and even back to my office, felt very awkward and uncertain. My journal entry of February 18, 1991, is revealing.

> *This will be my week of reentry. Buelah will start back to work the following week. I wonder if I'll have to recite again what happened to everyone who asks. Can I really do it? It seems that I'll be recycling old grief, opening up the old wound again. I don't mind telling my friends, but my life is so public here, and so many want to know. I read an old African proverb that says, "Sorrow is a precious treasure, shared only with friends." That's the way I feel.*

Looking back, I realize that I probably should not have tried to do so much within such a short time. It was less than two weeks after the funeral that I attended my first staff meeting. In those days, staff meetings were conducted on the campus of the nearby university in the President's Dining Room. We normally sat around a large table, enjoyed a meal together, then got down to the business at hand.

My journal entry of February 18 reveals what happened during the mid-afternoon break.

As I walked across the dining room and saw the college students, I was overcome with the thought that Denny would not be among them any longer, would not graduate, marry, or have children. Seeing the students in all their happiness got to me, and I started to cry in the middle of the dining hall. Someone led me into the President's Dining Room, where I continued to cry for some time. Pastor Paul laid his hands on me, explained to the others what had happened, and prayed for me. I left through the back door, crying. With tears, hardly able to see, I drove to the cemetery and spent some time near Denny's grave. Later, I went back to my office and cried some more.

Not only did we have staff meetings on the campus, but I was also an adjunct professor and taught two classes in addition to my duties at the church. When

I returned to the classroom and tried to resume my teaching schedule, sitting in front of me was Denny's best friend, Greg. It was a small class, and I had already chosen to sit with them in a circle of chairs. I could not escape the shocked and haunting look in his eyes as I tried to teach.

I tried putting the class at ease by telling them the truth about my feelings. I felt it was best to be up-front with them so they would understand if I had to suddenly excuse myself and run to the nearest restroom and cry for a few minutes. I'm not sure how much I was able to teach them. But across the years I have received several affirming letters from many of the students in that class. They may have signed up for a course in adult Christian education, but they also experienced a grief laboratory as well.

Buelah returned to work a few days after I returned to my office, and her reentry was no easier than mine. She worked in the church office and spent much of her time in the copy room, working with the machines that printed the weekly bulletins and folded and addressed them. Above the machines where she worked was a window that faced out over the parking lot of the church. Since our sanctuary was large enough to easily accommodate the student body of the nearby university, they attended their weekly chapel services there, and she could glance out the window and watch the students driving into the parking lot to attend the services.

Quite often she had noticed our son's dark blue four-by-four Toyota truck as he turned into a parking space. It was a warm and happy sight for her to see him coming to chapel at the university he loved. After his death, she would stand by the folding machine, staring out the window with tears in her eyes as she scanned the parking lot, hoping to see him pull up in his dark blue Toyota pick-up. She would never see it again.

In those first months after Denny's death, I was beginning to see new ways in which the church could acknowledge the grief of our members who had suffered losses. At that time, we were not doing much to help grievers as we approached special days on the church calendar. I began to press the idea of creating new ways we could help acknowledge the grief of our people.

I recall the staff meeting where I suggested we do something special for the grievers in our candlelight Communion service. This is usually the Sunday just before Christmas, and the service is held at night. The sanctuary is tastefully decorated with green wreaths and red ribbons. The powerful ceiling lights are left off with the only source of light coming from thousands of candles. On that special night there's a feeling of hushed holiness in our 4,000-seat sanctuary. While families may sit apart at other worship times, on this night they sit together—grandparents, parents, and children. The orchestra accompanies the 100-voice choir as they sing the wonderful songs of Christmas. At the close, we celebrate Holy Communion and then finish by singing "Silent Night" together.

As we were planning this service in our staff meeting, my suggestion was to give special recognition to grievers near the conclusion of this service. I thought this could be done after everyone had taken Communion. I suggested the pastor call attention to the special unlit candle at the front of the church. I went on to say that he could say some words about those among us who are grieving the death of a loved one. I thought it would be appropriate for someone to step forward while the pastor was speaking and light the center candle that had been previously unlit. This candle would be symbolic of those whom we have loved and lost by death.

The pastor and staff thought this was a good idea. They also wanted Buelah, Andy, and me to be the appointed ones to light this special candle.

I remember that service very well. Everything was beautiful in the sanctuary, and we had a great crowd that night. After the music and Communion, we neared the time when the candle of remembrance was to be lit. I reached under the pew where we were seated and pulled out the long brass candle-lighter. I quickly struck a match, lit the wick, and prepared to walk forward with Buelah and Andrew. The candle was on a pedestal, just inside the altar and near the Communion table. The three of us together held the brass candle lighter and lit the candle while the senior pastor was talking.

Then the pastor invited everyone who was grieving a loved one to walk forward and stand with us around the front of the altar. I remember standing there with my family, wondering if anyone would acknowledge their grief by coming forward to join us. After all, we had never done this before, and I was beginning to think how silly we would look if no one came forward to be with us. A guitarist was nearby, sitting on a stool, leading the congregation in the song "Silent Night," and my fears were growing with each phrase we sang.

Then, before we came to the words "sleep in heavenly peace" there were people walking down every aisle, many of them with tears streaming down their faces. It was as though a gate had been suddenly opened and we were giving them permission to mourn their losses. I estimate that there were more than 150 people standing with us by the time the song finished. While the pastor prayed the benediction on the service, I could hear people sobbing softly across the front of the church. I was among those who cried as I had the opportunity to express how sad I was. Afterward, the senior pastor came to me and said, "We need to do this every year."

We haven't missed a year since then. Through the years I have taken the lead and asked different ones to light that special candle. We always go forward with the other grievers, because we still miss him and are glad the church allows space in the Christmas Communion service where we not only follow the instructions of Jesus to remember Him, but we also remember others whom we love.

The church I serve has been a place of great support and great pain. We were tempted to sell our home and get out of town, away from all the painful reminders. We had the opportunity, and we gave it serious thought. Within two weeks of our son's death, I received a telephone call from a district superintendent in Florida. He asked if I would be willing to fly down and interview at one of his churches on that district. My first impulse was to say I would and to consider this as a wonderful opportunity to get away from the house where Denny had died. No one would blame us if we wanted to get as far away as possible from the painful reminders.

I asked him if he knew that we had recently lost our son. He said he did not, and he expressed his deep sympathy to me over the phone. Then I told him that I couldn't leave this town yet. I instinctively knew it would be a mistake for us to leave our church and community. Looking back, I'm thankful that, in spite of my shock, God gave me the wisdom to know it would be unwise to leave.

While the church was at times a place of awful pain for us, it was also the place of comfort and support. After all, these were the people who knew our son and the stories about him. In the days ahead, we would need to hear those stories. The people in Florida had never met him. I can only imagine the disaster that would have followed if we had gone to Florida and pretended as though nothing were wrong. I'm glad we stayed. This church is our home.

EIGHT

I DIDN'T CRY
THIS MORNING

4/7/91

I often wonder if we'll ever feel happy again. When I walked into the church foyer tonight before the service, I saw a group of people laughing. I was glad they could do that, but envious too. I can't see us doing that anytime soon.

5/4/91

This morning we sat in an orientation session designed to get students ready for the exchange program. It was helpful, and we enjoyed it very much. Afterward, the three of us had lunch at the Olive Garden restaurant. We soon noticed after we had sat down at the table that we had a very special waitress. She was special because she was very precise and didn't make a mistake, always doing exactly the right thing, like a robot. We got tickled as we overheard her talking to the people at a nearby table. She was telling them to be careful of the moisture caused by condensation on the underneath side of the plate. Buelah especially got tickled and laughed until she cried. Then she caught herself and said, "That is the first time I've really laughed in three months." I noticed it, too, even before she said it. I think today was a turning point, and she's on her way back. Thank God.

During my lifetime I have endured a few severe winters. These were the winters when the wind was bitter-cold, when several days passed without the appearance of the sun. The snowfall was extremely heavy, and travel was difficult. During those winters, I eagerly anticipated and looked forward to the first signs of spring. As we approached the end of February and rolled into March, I knew the signs to look for. We have a tulip bed in our front yard, and as I pulled out of the driveway each morning, I took a quick look at it, wondering when those first green shoots would push through the soil and appear. When I saw these first signs of spring, I knew it wouldn't be long until I would see the color of springtime once again. I gained hope from those green shoots, because I knew what would follow.

Every newly bereaved person I talk with always wants to know how long his or her pain will continue, how long his or her bitter winter of sorrow will last. It's a natural question to ask. After all, grieving is the hardest work we do, and it's only natural to want to know "When do I get a break from this?" The soul-crushing weight of grief is almost more than a person can bear, and we often wonder if the day will ever come when we'll smile or laugh again. Then, when we do start to get a "break" from our pain, we often feel guilty. This is the paradox to grieving that is often misunderstood. Sometimes we don't want our grief to be taken from us, because the grieving itself is a connection between us and our dead child.

As mentioned earlier, we were in severe shock during those first few days and weeks. After a while, we would have brief moments when we actually thought we were getting over it—hope springs eternal. You can see from the following entry that I was hoping we could escape the horrible pain we were feeling.

3/12/91

Today has been a good day, maybe because I've had my mind on other things for a while, such as the martin house Kenny gave me. It seems I can go a few hours without thinking about Denny and actually enjoy myself. Then I'll see something on TV or think of something that reminds me so much of him, and once again I feel the pain and feel the weight of his loss. It's still very hard to believe. Tonight we went to an activity at church and had a good time. I think we're getting better. We mingled with the others, didn't cry, and had a good time. Tomorrow we'll attend a grief workshop. It will be interesting to see how it goes. I hope it helps.

It's probably a good thing I didn't know how long our winter of grief would continue, because it was much longer than I expected. Along the way, there have been times when I would get a glimmer of hope that we might survive it. Let me tell you about the signs I noticed in my life.

In the beginning, the pain was overwhelming and unbelievable. Denny had died on the couch in our family room, and I tried to stay away from that room, even though it was the most popular room in our home. My journal entry of 2/17/91, just eleven days after he died, describes the feeling I had toward that room:

Denny died in the family room—how fitting for our boy to die there since he loved his family so much. The family room was a place of warmth, pillows, blankets, friends, plants, and love. But now it's different. It seems cold, dark, and sullen. I have trouble staying in the family room for any period of time—10 minutes is long enough. I wonder how long it will be until I can look at the couch and not see his body, still and lifeless. I still can't believe it.

In order to make my way to the garage where the car was kept, I had to walk close to the very place where he had taken his last breath. It took a while, but finally I was able to do it without seeing him on our couch. Only God knows how much I've grieved in that room and all the memories associated with it. Looking back, I know it was the right thing for us to grieve in that room until the cup of sorrow was fully drained.

There was one particular experience of grieving in the family room that I can share here. A few years ago our friend Harold Ivan Smith was at the Crystal Cathedral in Garden Grove, California, the guest of Robert Schuller on the "Hour of Power." It was just before Christmastime, and Dr. Schuller had invited him so that he could be interviewed and talk about his book, *A Decembered Grief.* When Harold returned to Kansas City from taping the program, he told me about his experience at the Crystal Cathedral and also mentioned the date it would be televised locally. He also asked if he could come to our home so we could see the show together.

It was a cold December Sunday morning when we all gathered in our family room to watch. Mary Margaret

Reed was a weekend guest in our home, and the four of us watched the show with anticipation, wondering how the interview with Dr. Schuller would turn out. That particular program was stunning. It began with a series of Christmas carols, complete with the smiling faces of children singing in a special choir. I sat by the fire drinking a hot cup of coffee when it came time for the interview.

Dr. Schuller held up Harold's book for all to see, and I was glad Harold was getting the recognition he deserved for writing this important book. At one point he asked Harold an interesting question: "Harold, many years ago you were here at Crystal Cathedral as a special speaker to our single adults. In those days you were writing and speaking exclusively to single adults across the country. What caused you to change over from single adult ministry to grief and bereavement issues?"

I'll never forget the moment or the place I was sitting in our family room when Harold answered Dr. Schuller by saying, "It was the death of a teenage boy named Denny that effected this shift in my career."

When I heard Harold Ivan's answer to Dr. Schuller, I nearly dropped my coffee cup! In an instant, tears were running down my face. I looked over at Buelah, and she, too, was wiping away her tears. Then I looked at Harold Ivan and could not help but notice the significance of the place where he was sitting: on the same couch and in the exact place where our son had taken his last breath. In that moment I was glad we had not moved away but were able—with Harold Ivan's help—to take this painful location and start to "reframe" it.

Across the years, I've watched as several people have sold their homes and moved away from the painful places, away from their painful reminders. If anyone asks me, I always encourage them to stay where they are and not run away from these painful reminders. It will get better if you're patient.

I can now see several signs—green shoots—that gave me reason to believe I could actually survive this catastrophe and go on. As mentioned earlier, weddings were so painful that we simply stayed away for fear our tears would be too much of a distraction. We even received a handwritten note from one of Denny's former girlfriends inviting us to attend her wedding. We simply couldn't do it. However, there did come a day when weddings were not as painful as they had been.

I think of one wedding in particular in which I was asked to officiate. It was a very large one, and most of my son's friends were in the wedding party. The ceremony was stunning, and we had a wonderful time celebrating together. Later, after I arrived at home and started to take off my tie, I had a moment to reflect on what had just happened that afternoon. It was one of those moments when I realized I had just officiated at a wedding that included most of my son's closest friends and that I had actually had a wonderful time. I did not cry, nor did I have the overwhelming sadness and sorrow such as I had experienced before.

In the privacy of my bedroom, I placed both hands on the dresser and made an altar of it as I thanked God for the progress I was making. It was a special moment when I knew I was getting better. The date was July 15, 1995, about four and a half years after the death of our son.

The next things I noticed were the photographs. While I was in heavy shock, I could look at his photograph as I mourned for him. By the way, I've observed how families will run to the photo albums and pull out the shots of the deceased immediately after he or she has died. Part of this photo-gathering is to prepare a video memorial for the visitation and funeral service. However, a few weeks after the funeral, it was simply too painful for me to look at Denny's photos.

Also, whenever we traveled to visit my parents, my eyes stayed away from the photos of Denny when I walked through the front door. Looking at them was almost like walking into the funeral home and seeing his body in the casket. It was a horrible reminder of what had happened, and I couldn't bring myself to face it. My wife felt the same way and had difficulty looking at the photos of him when he was younger. The Christmas ones of him and his brother on Santa's knee were too much to handle, so the first Christmas—10 months after his death—was more than we could bear. We didn't get them out that year. I can't find much record of this in my journal, but I'm quite certain it was years before I could look at his photo without feeling a twinge of pain.

It may take years before the green shoots of hope begin to appear in your life. Again, be patient and keep looking for them. They'll reappear after your long winter of grief.

Below is a list of signs that will help you recognize that you're getting better:

1. You don't feel compelled to tell everyone—even strangers—about the death of your child.

2. You don't cry yourself to sleep every night.

3. You sleep well and can awaken feeling rested.

4. You can walk past his or her room and not be reduced to tears.

5. You can go to the grocery store and not be upset when you see his or her favorite food on the shelf.

6. Your food starts to taste good again, and your appetite returns.

7. You have the desire to get out of bed and face the day.

8. You can walk or drive past the place where he or she died and not be consumed by the pain of your loss.

9. You're no longer overwhelmed with sadness when you hear the lyrics to certain songs.

10. You can place flowers on his or her grave and not be overcome with sadness.

11. It becomes easier to face his or her birth and death dates on the calendar.

12. You really do want to try to live again.

13. You enjoy going to the place of worship and begin to feel renewed in your soul.

14. You start noticing flowers, birds, the sky, and all living things in a new way.

15. You have a strong desire to redeem your child's death by using it to help others.

16. You start to take an interest in a hobby or an interest you had before your child died.

17. You have empathy for someone else who's suffering a hardship.

18. Your short-term memory starts to gradually return.

19. You can look at your child's picture and remember the good times instead of the pain of his or her death.

20. You can talk with others about your child and laugh about the funny and interesting things he or she did.

21. You look forward and plan for the holidays instead of dreading them.

22. You can go to favorite restaurants and eat without thinking of the empty chair and the person who used to sit across from you.

23. You can attend the milestone functions of your child's friends and actually be happy for them instead of crying over what you'll never have.

24. You can look at other people's children and grandchildren and actually be happy for the parents and grandparents.

25. You have forgiven—or are trying to forgive—the person you feel is responsible for your son's death.

26. You can forgive yourself for things you said or things you should have said and didn't.

27. You have forgiven God for not stepping in and saving your child's life.

28. You have forgiven your child for his or her part in the death, especially if the child died by suicide.

29. You catch yourself singing once again.

30. You cherish your family and friends in a new way and find new ways to express your love for them.

When I was a young boy, I was riding my bicycle one summer day with some other friends when the front wheel skidded on some loose gravel, and I went down in a dusty crash. As I was falling, I instinctively placed my right hand out in order to break the fall. Along the road there were some sharp stubs sticking up like the tips of tiny spears. They were as sharp as razors. One of these sharp stubs ripped open a large gash on my hand, and I instantly began to cry out in pain. My hand was very bloody as I got up and ran toward the house to find my mother. She realized it was serious and quickly took me to the doctor. I still recall the horrible pain I felt and my screams as the doctor cleaned out the wound and then closed it up with 12 stitches.

After the doctor bandaged up my hand and the tears had dried, I was taken out for ice cream. I held my hand up above my heart because of the throbbing pain I felt when I let it fall to my side. Over the next several days, I babied my hand, making sure it was protected at night while I slept, and I made sure no one got too close to it when I was awake. My usual activities were changed. I couldn't play baseball or ride a bike, and I even had to eat with my left hand. Someone had to help me dress, undress, and tie my shoes.

At the end of 10 days, I returned to the doctor's office to have the bandages and stitches removed. My mother had to practically drag me back there. I had experienced too much pain in that place to go willingly. We sat in the doctor's office for what seemed like a long time, and I was quite nervous when they called me into the examining room. The smell of alcohol and adhesive raised my anxiety even more as we waited for the doctor to appear. My hand was still very sensitive, and I didn't want anyone to touch it. When the doctor came in, he sat down, took my hand, and carefully cut off the blood-soaked bandages to inspect the cut and remove the stitches.

I watched with great fear as he took his needle-nosed scissors and began to cut each stitch, one at a time, until he had cut all of them. Then—and this was the worst part—he took tweezers and began to pull each stitch out of my hand. Tears came to my eyes, and I screamed out in pain as he removed each one. He then placed another bandage on my hand and ordered me to be careful and not use the hand for several more days. Finally the whole ordeal was over, and I was very relieved. Mom and I made our way to the ice cream store once again.

Over the next few days, weeks, and months, it seemed to my young mind that my wound would never heal. It was frustrating not being able to play baseball or ride my bike. In fact, that red bike sat in the garage for quite some time before I wanted to ride it again. There was just too much pain associated with it.

Once in a while when doing something in the house, I would forget and bump my hand on something. I would be in tears, hoping I hadn't torn the wound open again. Gradually—ever so gradually—I began to use my injured hand once again to throw a ball, swing the bat, and even ride my bike. It took a long time, but it did finally heal, and today I can use my right hand as well as my left.

As I type these words, I've taken the time to lift my hand from the keyboard and reflect on that long, ugly scar. The scar will be with me until I die. If by some chance I'm in a horrible accident and someone needs to identify my body, they can just look at the palm of my right hand. It will always be there.

In much the same way, the pain of our child's death has ripped us open, causing a nearly mortal wound. As my friend said to me, "You've had your heart ripped out of you, without the aid of a general anesthetic." We're staggered by this wound and are trying to get along the best we can, hoping we can live through the pain. We learn to make adjustments, realizing that everything has changed and that we'll have to search for or create new normalcy. Gradually—ever so gradually—a scab will form over the once-bleeding wound, and we'll find new ways to cope, to go on.

Since Denny's death almost 17 years ago, I've had

several people ask, "Do you ever get over it?" I always answer by telling them, "No, you never get over it. It gets different, but you never get over it." For us, the first five years represent the worst of the nightmare. We'll have a big scar on our hearts forever.

NINE

I'M BEGINNING
TO LIVE AGAIN

8/26/91, 11:40 P.M.

As I read the Psalm 102, I was struck by verse 9, when David cried out, especially the part about mingling his tears and drink. I remember the first Communion I helped serve after Denny's death. Dan and I served from the Communion table that sat exactly where Denny's casket had been during the funeral service. As I took the tray of cups and prepared to hand it to the servers, my brother Scott stood up and started singing a Communion song.

Suddenly I was remembering the death of two sons—God's and mine. The place, the event, Scott's music—he sang at Denny's funeral—were too much to handle. A rush of tears came down my cheeks, and I couldn't hide them. My hands were full of Communion trays, symbolizing the blood of Christ, and my tears of sorrow over the loss of my son were mingling with the symbolic blood.

I thought about that symbolism today. The cup reminds us of the blood, the powerful blood of Jesus. Because He gave, we have received. However, that night I was also serving my tears, symbolic of the terrible pain I was feeling. Perhaps because of Denny's death we can help others who need help as much. Then, through my speaking, writing, counseling, perhaps through my tears, others may gain some hope and courage. The symbolism of all this is almost overwhelming to me. I'll never forget the night when I served Christ's blood—and my tears.

She sat in front of my desk. We had already talked about the weather and other items of general interest. I knew why she was there, but I asked her. "Tell me what brought you here to my office today." I looked at her sad eyes, and she asked the question I've heard so many times from those who have lost a child by death: "How can I reclaim myself, and how long will this last?" Her teenage son had been murdered just a few weeks prior, and I knew she was in agony, wondering how long she could go on like this.

I wanted to tell her of a secret shortcut or say something that would relieve her of the nightmare she was living. I wanted to pray a special prayer that would instantly grant her the comfort she was hoping for. But

I had to tell her the truth: "This will take a long, long time, and you'll struggle to find a new normalcy." I went on to tell her there were some things she could do in order to reclaim herself.

Since my son's death, countless people have come to me for counseling, because, as one man said, "You know what real pain is all about." I'll be the first to admit that I can't possibly know what other people are experiencing. I only know my own pain and can say with certainty that I've experienced a depth of suffering that I did not know existed prior to my son's death. There's certainly no quick fix or remedy for this type of broken heart.

Having said that, I often share with others some things I believe will be of help to them as they move along their grief path. There are a number of things grievers can do as they try to reconcile themselves to the pain they're experiencing.

Therapist or Counselor

Sometimes the sadness and sorrow are so over-whelming that a person—or the family—feels the need to see a mental health professional for some additional help. It's best to not wait until there's a crisis before turning to a professional. If you feel your grief pattern is not normal, seek out a third party or a trusted friend, and ask for honest feedback. Early detection is always a good idea. Seeking outside help is not a sign of weakness but is an indication of strength and wisdom.

I receive calls nearly every day from people in our church and community asking me for the name of a Christian counselor, someone to whom they can turn. I try to be sensitive to their need but also remind them that the first question they must ask is whether or not this person is competent. I would say the same thing about my choice of an airline pilot to take me on my next trip. It would be nice to have a Christian pilot, but my first concern is about his or her competency as a pilot.

You can ask your friends or pastor for a recommendation if you don't have a therapist in mind. Don't overlook your funeral director when searching for a good grief counselor. Most funeral directors can be of great help in referring you to a competent grief counselor. In addition, he or she will probably have other resources, such as lending libraries, where you can obtain helpful books and DVDs.

Here are some of the things to look for when selecting a therapist: His or her level of education, years of experience, and experience with grief issues. Does he or she believe in "brief counseling," as one counselor bragged to me, or does he or she allow the griever the necessary time to process thoughts and feelings? Does the counselor highly recommend drugs, or is this something held back as a last resort? Does the counselor try to fix you quickly and move you on, or does he or she acknowledge your loss in a sensitive way that allows you to be the one who sets the pace of your therapy? These are just some of the many questions you should ask and have answered as you prepare to work one-on-one with a counselor.

Often the help you need can be found in your own church. Many churches have people who are specially trained to deal with grief issues in a one-on-one, confidential way. If you don't have such a ministry in your own church, check with other churches of your community. One that I can recommend is Stephen Ministries, found at <http://www.stephenministries.org>. You'll find it to be a wonderful and compassionate organization. They will make every attempt to assist you in finding someone who will meet with you regularly and walk with you through your time of sorrow.

Your pastor may be another resource, especially if he or she has suffered the loss of someone too. Beware of those who try to give you a quick fix with some Bible verses, telling you how a good Christian ought to grieve. A wise pastor will respect you and your grief journey, asking good questions and allowing you to express what you're feeling as you move along on your journey. A seasoned pastor will allow you the freedom to question your faith or express your anger toward God.

A key to your recovery will come as your counselor or pastor acknowledges your grief and steps into your story with you, feeling some of your pain. If you see tears in the eyes of the person who is listening to your grief story, chances are that you have a good listener in front of you. Stick with that person, even if he or she does not have an impressive degree on the wall.

Support Groups

As mentioned earlier, my wife and I learned about The Compassionate Friends (TCF), a support group that was established for bereaved parents. At our first meeting, we walked into the room and almost instantly felt at home, knowing there were others there who were dealing with the same type of pain we were experiencing. In those days, smoking was allowed in the meetings, and that finally drove us away. These days, it's rare to find groups where smoking is allowed. I heartily endorse TCF and groups like it—safe places for people like us who are looking for help in putting the pieces back together.

Most of my ministry since my son died has been in this area of starting and maintaining support groups. Now, more than ever, I seem to understand the importance of creating safe places where people can have their losses acknowledged in the context of a small group.

It wasn't many weeks after Denny died that my job description at the church changed, and I found myself working in the "recovery ministry." Part of my new assignment was to train leaders, start new support groups, and make sure they were running effectively—most important, to create safe places for all who wanted to attend. I took on the leadership of the grief group, knowing I needed help as much, if not more, than others in the group. Very early in my experience, I learned some hard lessons about support groups. Let me share some of them.

First, it's of great value if the leader has gone through this same experience. It's a rare person who has not lost a child who can lead a support group for bereaved parents. The leader will have much more credibility if he or she knows the feelings parents experience after learning their child has died.

It's important that respect is extended to the griever's individual pace. There are no clear-cut steps with which we move along on this grief journey. Beware of those who try to place you at a certain stage or step. I believe more harm has been done by those who try to force grievers into certain categories of grief. A good support group will allow you to simply be there and say nothing if you so choose.

I recall one eight-week group I conducted. One of the

157

participants did not say one word the entire eight weeks. I was a bit confused as to why she attended the group but did not talk. It was a bit unusual, but I commended her for showing up each week. In a few weeks I offered the same group again, and once again, she signed up. Finally, one evening during the second cycle, she spoke up and contributed to the conversation of the group.

After the group had ended that night, I asked if I could talk with her for a moment. "Donna, I noticed you didn't say one word in the previous support group, but tonight you opened up and talked freely. Why didn't you say anything in the previous group?"

She looked at me with sad eyes and said, "I was in so much pain during the first group, I couldn't say a word. I was afraid I might start crying and never be able to stop." She didn't need to say more. I understood and was glad I had not said anything to her before but instead respected her privacy and allowed her to progress at her own pace.

Another sign that a group is healthy has to do with the conduct of the facilitator. If he or she does most of the talking, be cautious. A good facilitator will ask the right questions and will model good listening.

In many support groups I have visited or known about, there's a tendency for either the facilitator or someone in the group to try to "fix" someone else in the group. For example, a group member may be totally frustrated and angry with God over the loss of her child and wants to know why this has happened. Quite often, in church-related support groups, there will be those who spring into action by quoting Bible verses to the person who's asking the question, thinking they'll be able to come up with some sort of "Bible" answer as to why the person's child was taken. A wise facilitator will discourage this sort of "fixing" right from the beginning by having in place the "no fixing" rule.

Watch for the amount of attention given to the matter of confidentiality. Strict confidentiality guidelines will help keep the group safe—"What is said here stays here."

Below is a complete list of the rules we have in place for our support groups. It's essential that we keep the groups safe for everyone.

Rules for Healthy Small-Group Discussion

1. While others are talking, please let them finish without interruption.
2. Speaking briefly and listening attentively are expected so that everyone has a chance to participate.
3. No fixing. We are here to listen, to support, and to be supported by each other in the group. We will listen to you, but please remember that there are others here who need to share as well.

4. Speak in the "I" form. Talk about how something or someone made you feel. (Example: "I felt sad when . . .")

5. Try to share from your heart as honestly as you can. It's OK to cry, laugh, be angry, or even be silent in the group without being condemned by others.

6. What is said in the group stays in the group. Anonymity is a basic requirement.

Journaling

Journaling was one of the disciplines that helped in my grief journey. Prior to my son's death, I had heard of others who kept either a diary or journal of their own grief experience. The very next day after my son's death, I found an old spiral notebook and began my journey with the journal. I recorded my feelings and activities for almost five years and kept every one of these notebooks in a storage closet. Somehow, the very act of journaling was therapeutic for me as I faithfully recorded the events of the day and the feelings associated with them. I kept my journal on my bedside table, and each night before turning out the lights, I took out the notebook, picked up a pen, and started writing. Now, as I review my journal entries, I can easily see the pattern I followed.

First, I wrote about what had happened that day— what I had been doing. Then it often went to what I was feeling. Often my wife would be crying into her pillow as

I wrote. Her crying often frustrated me, but I dared not say anything or try to "fix" her. The journal was a way to get at my feelings and put them onto paper. Again, it was my lifesaver. I encourage all grievers to try it, either on paper in a notebook or on a good software program. There are several to choose from.

Poetry

When a child is lost by death, there's something inside us that calls us to our own form of mourning. Sometimes it's through music, such as Eric Clapton did when he wrote "Tears in Heaven" after the loss of his small child, Conor. This tragedy happened only a few days after my own son died, so I've tracked with Clapton and his music, sometimes borrowing his mournful lyrics to help with my own mourning.

In addition to journaling, I found a special form of poetry to be helpful in getting at my feelings without the clutter of too many words. My wife and I have used the Japanese haiku as a way to express our grief. A haiku is a three-line poem with a syllable pattern of five, seven, five. Some haiku are written in four lines. The important thing to remember is that the first and last lines each have five syllables. All the words in between, whether written as one or two lines, contain seven syllables. In other words, the haiku is a way of putting a frame around an experience.

Whether you're writing a haiku about a past or present event, you stand still and enter into the experience. This is a way of immortalizing a moment in time. The question to ask as you write your haiku is *What do I see, and how can I express what I see?* Writing your haiku is like painting a picture with only a few words. In creating your haiku, strive to say what you see in the simplest way possible. Here below is a sampling of mine:

February fog
bringing painful memories
to my broken heart

I saw the blue truck
like the one he used to drive
moving without him.

I see his picture
and I think of other times
when he would say, "Hello, Dad"
and give me a hug

Each of these poems creates a visual image of a memory from my past grief. The haiku is one way to get at my feelings and succinctly express my feelings when I see fog in February, a blue Toyota pickup, or his photograph.

After sharing my poetry with Buelah, she also tried

her hand at doing the same. When I described the five, seven, five syllables to her, she told me one morning she awakened in bed and began to tap out the syllables on her pillow case as she had strong thoughts about Denny. When she had one she liked, she quickly jumped out of bed, found a pen and pad, and jotted it down for safe-keeping. Below are some of her haiku:

> The sadness is great
> The grief is overwhelming
> But still we go on

> March one is the date
> Dennis Alan came to us
> He was a wonderful gift
> He brought us such joy

> February six
> A dark day we remember
> He left us too soon

There are many who would think this exercise morbid. If you feel it will be helpful to you, do not let their feelings about it discourage you. I encourage you to write about your experiences using the haiku and then share them with someone who understands. The treasure you have within your memories will soon become apparent as you get in touch with your deeper feelings. You'll be surprised at the help you'll receive when some-

one else acknowledges your feelings as you read your poetry to him or her.

Of course, our son Andy was also deeply affected by his brother's death. Soon after Denny died, he said to me, "When Denny died, I lost my best friend." It wasn't long until Andy also used poetry to help express the deep sorrow he felt. Below is the first poem he wrote:

A Tribute

The last time I cried

Was when my brother died.

I expect to see him when I look in his room,

But he has met his final doom.

His future was so bright,

But God decided to take him from our sight.

He almost died two years before,

But this time he passed through heaven's door.

Why did he have to be taken away?

I hope I will see him again someday.

He was so special to me, more so than any other;

I was proud to tell anyone, "He's my big brother."

Physical Exercise

When the heart is deeply wounded, there's a tendency to pull in and stay to oneself. This is the body's normal response, to be still and try to recover. Getting

out for a walk or some other form of exercise can seem like an impossible task.

Before he died, Denny had been heavily involved in running, swimming, and bike riding, all of which are included in triathalons. We had watched him compete many times. It seemed natural for us to take up bike riding and running and walking as well. Looking back, I think we both felt somewhat closer to him as we rode our bikes together. It became one of the things we did in order to get needed exercise. It was not unusual for Buelah and me to ride several miles for a meal and talk together as we rode.

7/29/91

We got out of bed around 9:00 and rode our bikes to Stanley, where we ate breakfast at McDonald's. A lovely day with the temps at 75-80 degrees. We are both tired but had a wonderful day. Buelah acts so much like her old self.

I encourage fresh grievers to go for a walk every day. If necessary, take someone else along. It was on some of my long walks that I had some wonderful thoughts come to me about Denny, my life, and what I might be doing with this tragedy.

2/27/91

I took a walk by myself tonight. A full moon lit my way, and it was a bit warmer tonight. As I walked I heard geese honking. I looked up and could see the flying "V" formation as they headed north. They have a God-given instinct to fly north when warmer weather is imminent. God has also placed a compulsion in my heart to take the brokenness from Denny's death and turn it into something good, something helpful for someone somewhere. I will not let his death be the final word.

Books

Both my wife and I love to read and have often discussed how impoverished our lives would be were it not for the help we received from our books. They are like old and trusted friends. As mentioned before, I was so angry with God that I ignored the reading of the Scriptures for a long time. I turned instead to other books such as *Disappointment with God* and Kushner's *When Bad Things Happen to Good People*. I was on a search, trying to find some meaning in the tragedy that had entered our lives.

While both of these volumes were interesting and helpful, I soon came across other books that were of more help to me. I read several books written by other dads who had lost children. One of the most meaningful ones was written by another pastor, John Claypool. He wrote the book *Tracks of a Fellow Struggler*. There were several others, but the ones that helped me most were the ones that led me to feel a connection with the author through our shared experience of suffering the loss of a child. After reading certain books, I felt as though I had been in the best support group in town. It was a comforting feeling.

Using Your Grief to Make a Difference

In 1980 Candy Lightner, the founder of Mothers Against Drunk Drivers (MADD), lost her 13-year-old daughter when she was hit by a drunken hit-and-run driver. Candy vowed she would not let her daughter's death be in vain, and she started this single-issue organization. In 1983 a television movie gave her organization national exposure, and it began to grow rapidly.

The group had its greatest success with the imposition of a 1984 federal law that required states to raise the minimum legal age for purchase and possession of alcohol to 21 or lose federal highway funding. Candy is a great example of a parent taking tragedy and using it to bring a needed change in our world.

Another person who chose to take his tragedy and accomplish something positive from it is Gordon Smith, senator from Oregon. After the suicide of his son Garrett, Smith was able to successfully push through legisla-

tion—the Garrett Lee Smith Memorial Act—in which $82
million in grants was authorized to help prevent suicide
by young people. This will enable schools to have money, among other things, earmarked for mental health
screenings. Smith used his private pain to bring about
needed change and improvement in detecting mental
illness among our nation's students.

My Story

As you can see from the journal entry at the beginning
of this chapter, it was in August 1991 while serving Holy
Communion at the altar of our church that I began to feel
stirrings to use my personal tragedy to help others. It was
a very emotional time as I began to sense a special mis-
sion before me. I didn't realize it then, but now I can see
that God has used our tragedy to bring about something
new in our church. I referred to some of these in other
places, but here are the changes that have been made in
our church as a result of Denny's death:

1. Memorial poinsettias at Christmastime with
   names of the deceased printed for all to see in
   the worship folder.

2. Memorial lilies at Easter time, following the
   same pattern as Christmas.

3. Special memorial service at Christmas, "A Time
   to Remember," as family and friends have opportunity to remember their loved ones.

4. Support groups for parents who have lost children by death.

5. Support groups for those who have lost loved ones by death.

6. Support groups such as divorce recovery, and others.

7. Special remembrance ribbons worn on Mother's Day by those who have lost their mothers.

8. Special remembrance ribbons worn on Father's Day by those who have lost their fathers.

9. Legacy web site for family or friends to post photographs and stories of those they have lost by death. As mentioned earlier, you can access our church's Legacy web site by going to <www.ccnlegacy.org>.

10. The ritual of the "unlit candle of remembrance" when we have the annual candlelight Communion service at Christmastime.

These are just a few of the things we now practice at the church where I serve. All of them have come about since the death of our son. This is the message of the Cross, to take the worst that has happened to us and turn it into something good. As we do this, we will not only remember our child but will start to reclaim ourselves in the process.

10

A WOUNDED HEALER?

2/5/96

Today is my day off, a day of recovery from the ski trip but also the day before, THE DAY, February 6. Five years ago tonight I said goodnight to my son Denny for the last time. I think I said, "I love you," before going upstairs to bed. With Andy doing homework at the kitchen table and Denny resting on the couch in the family room just a few feet away, everything seemed normal. The doctor said he could go on the ski trip, but all would change in just a few hours.

Tonight Andy called from Philly and talked to us for over 30 minutes. We both know why he called, and the three of us talked about what happened five years ago. I'm glad we're all able to remember, talk about it, and acknowledge it. For so long the pain was so great that we couldn't talk about it.

I have remembrances of Denny in unexpected places. Today, in the dentist's office, the assistant told me she knew Denny and that he was a friend of her friend, Scott. I looked at her and wondered where Denny would be in his career, in his life. When we arrived home yesterday we had a note from Harold Ivan. He has always remembered February 6 and been present for us.

This is an unusual and unsettling time for me. I have been feeling that something is going to happen, a new turn in my life. I'm aware, as I come to the end of this journal notebook, that a lot has happened since I started to journal on February 7, 1991. My life has been profoundly changed, and I'm trying to figure out what it all means. Where is this leading me? What does God expect of me? It seems I have more questions than answers, but I believe in a God who works with us in spite of our questions.

It was almost noon Tuesday, April 26, 1994, when I walked into the President's Dining Room at MidAmerica Nazarene University. Our pastoral staff was preparing to have lunch together and then conduct our customary business. We were having informal conversations around the table when I turned to our music director and asked him how the plans were coming along for the upcoming Sunday. I knew he had been planning for this important day, because it was graduation Sunday, the time when parents and friends would be in town for the annual commencement.

Bill was planning to present the musical "God with Us," and I knew the choir and orchestra had been working overtime to make it special for the expected 4,000 people in attendance. Bill turned to me and said he was almost ready but needed one more person to speak.

In the musical he was planning, there were two places where people who had experienced a personal crisis were supposed to give a testimony of how God had been with them, in keeping with the theme. Bill already had a dad lined up who had a wonderful answer to prayer, but he wanted one more person to speak—a person who didn't get the answer he or she wanted but was still trusting in God.

I remembered the story of the other family and the severe illness of their little seven-year-old girl. Her illness was due to a rare virus, and they had taken her to several specialists, but no one could find a way to help her. She became worse and was near death as she lay in the intensive care unit at a local hospital. Our church, along with several other churches, was asked to pray and fast, asking God to spare her life. Miraculously, she recovered, and everyone praised God for the way in which she had been healed. I was one of those who prayed for this little girl, even though I was still questioning if prayer was effective.

Bill turned to me and said, "Dennis, how about you? Will you share your story with the congregation and be the other person in this presentation?"

I was stunned and could hardly believe he was still looking for someone to speak only five days before the presentation was scheduled. He usually had these things planned several weeks in advance.

My first response was to tell him there was no way I would do it. I hadn't been honest with him or the rest of the staff about my hidden rift with God. My faith was paper thin, and I felt like the father who had taken his son to Jesus to be healed. Jesus had said to him, "Everything is possible for him who believes." Then the father said the words that best described my spiritual condition at that time: "I do believe; help me overcome my unbelief!" (Mark 9:23-24).

Bill saw my hesitation but would not take no for an answer. He was persistent, so I finally said I would think about it.

After the staff meeting I told Buelah about it, and her first response was similar to mine. However, after giving it more thought, I finally decided to do it. That following Sunday, May 1, 1994, was another one of those important times for me and my recovery journey. My journal entry of 5/1/94 tells the story:

We arrived at church, greeted people, and took a seat near the front of the sanctuary. Seated in front of me was another family. The father sat directly in front of me. Next to him was a little seven-year-old girl. I knew who this was. This was the little girl who almost died, but miraculously, God touched her and she recovered.

The service started, and I still didn't know exactly what I would say. The church was full with family and friends, in addition to the regulars. The other father was to speak first, and he did so with a written manuscript in front of him. He did a good job of telling the story, and at the end his little girl left her seat and joined him at the front of the church as everyone clapped.

The choir sang some more, and then it was my turn. I took the microphone, stood in front of the podium, and told our story. I was honest about my anger, prayerlessness, about feeling cheated, and told the stories in which these feelings were expressed. At the end I said, "When the graduates line up tomorrow, there will be one person missing, and I will grieve about our loss. However, God is with us. I know God is with us (I didn't always know that), and that we will be OK. When I finished I sat down to applause. People everywhere were crying, and it was a very emotional moment.

The choir sang some more, and then something unusual happened. People started moving toward the altars. The senior pastor took the microphone and gave an invitation for anyone who needed to pray. Several people were at the altar. I went forward to pray with a recovering alcoholic and his wife. Another unusual thing happened—hardly anyone left the church. After the altar services, people came to me, hugged me, and told me how much they appreciated me sharing our pain.

When I spoke to the church that day, I decided to come out of hiding and show my wounds, to be very candid about my struggle with God. I was so honest, in fact, that I thought the church board might ask for my resignation. I was not prepared for the response that followed that public confession. In the days, weeks, and even years since that service, I have had several hundred people come to me, telling about their disappointment with God, about their unanswered prayers, about their disillusion with God and questions about prayer. I heard stories of those who had had miscarriages; whose children had died; who had lost spouses, siblings, or parents; about bankruptcy, divorces, unemployment, and terminal illnesses. In addition, there were alcoholics; drug addicts; sex addicts; parents whose children were incarcerated; survivors of suicide. The number of people in our church who were grieving was unbelievable. I asked myself, *Were they always here and I simply didn't see them?*

Looking back, I think it was my own public confession, admitting to my brokenness and disappointment with God, my prayerlessness, lack of Bible reading, and even my anger toward God that gave other people the courage to approach me and tell their stories. As I listened, they seemed to be saying to me, "If you as one of our pastors feel this way, maybe it's OK for me to disclose my questions about God too."

After that service, my office phone began to ring more frequently than before as people made appointments with me in order to tell their stories. I often felt as though my office was a confessional as I sat and listened to them share their pain. I always made sure there was a large box of tissues on my desk. It was replenished frequently. We cried and grieved together. That pattern continues even to this day.

I began to understand the deep and painful truth of

Paul's writings when he said, "Praise be to the God and Father of our Lord Jesus Christ, the Father of compassion and the God of all comfort, who comforts us in all our troubles, so that we can comfort those in any trouble with the comfort we ourselves have received from God. For just as the sufferings of Christ flow over into our lives, so also through Christ our comfort overflows" (2 Cor. 1:3-5).

Brennan Manning in his book *Abba's Child* shares a wonderful story that has brought me comfort and meaning through these 17 years since Denny's death.

Thornton Wilder's one-act play "The Angel That Troubled the Waters," based on John 5:1-4, dramatizes the power of the pool of Bethesda to heal when an angel stirred its waters. A physician comes periodically to the pool, hoping to be the first in line and longing to be healed of his melancholy.

The angel finally appears but blocks the physician just as he's ready to step into the water. The angel tells the physician to draw back, for this moment is not for him. The physician pleads in a broken voice for help, but the angel insists that healing is not intended for him.

The dialogue continues—and then comes the prophetic word from the angel: "Without your wounds, where would your power be? It is your melancholy that makes your low voice tremble into the hearts of men and women. The very angels themselves cannot persuade the wretched and blundering children on earth as can one human being broken on the wheels of living. In Love's service, only wounded soldiers can serve. Physician, draw back."

Later, the man who enters the pool first and is healed rejoices in his good fortune, and turning to the physician says, "Please come with me. It is only an hour to my home. My son is lost in dark thoughts. I do not understand him and only you have ever lifted his mood. Only an hour. There is also my daughter: since her child died, she sits in the shadow. She will not listen to us but she will listen to you" (Brennan Manning, *Abba's Child* [Colorado Springs: NavPress, 1994], 24-25).

Looking back, I can see that my most effective days as a pastor started when I shared my wounds with those around me. I'm glad I took the risk and started telling the truth about my inward pain and especially my disappointment with God. By the way, whenever I come across a broken person, I encourage him or her to also be honest and open about the scars and the pain—to risk sharing that pain with others.

When Jesus appeared to His disciples, just after His resurrection, He said to Thomas, "Put your hand into my wounds and you will know who I am." (See John 20:27.) Jesus was identified by His wounds. He who overcame death, hell, and the grave still had the scars in His body. He could have shown His disciples a body that had no marks of His previous agony, but He chose to let them see these awful reminders of the price He paid.

Since Denny's death, my ministry has taken a new turn, and I have tried to follow my heart. Most of my ministry has been in "New Hope for Recovery." The New Hope ministry has touched thousands of lives with the various support groups that meet each week. Every week there are groups huddled together where they share their wounds with one another. We have taken a page from the Alcoholics Anonymous tradition in which the group members are encouraged to make their wounds visible.

Those who come to our groups are motivated by some awful pain in their lives. They often come to me or to our groups for a cure but are not always willing to expose their wounds, their pain. Gradually they often take courage from those of us who willingly allow our scars and wounds to be visible. These wounds need to be cleaned, but they can't be cleaned and given proper medication until we reveal them.

I recall a lady who came to one of our support groups. She had been sexually abused by members of her own family, and her shame was almost more than she could bear. As she began to hear the stories of others in her group, she also began to share small bits and pieces of her pain. She was in the shallow end of the pool but not quite ready to jump in completely.

Over the span of several months, she became bolder and took even more courage from the others in the group until one day she came out with the dark secrets that had haunted her. As she talked, she noticed the tears on the faces of others in the group, and that was a turning point in her healing. Today she can talk about her abuse in the same way she might talk about going to the store to pick up a gallon of milk.

It's difficult to sum up the ways in which my life has changed over these 17 years, but let me try to explain. These days my wife and I treat all our relationships much more carefully than before. We try not to miss a birthday, wedding, or anniversary celebration. My wife attends and has hosted dozens of wedding and baby showers. Also, we try to never miss a visitation, funeral, or memorial service. We celebrate Thanksgiving and Christmas in a big way, quite a contrast to the early years following Denny's death.

I have told several of my friends that we should be "loving the socks off one another." Little things that used to bother us are now trivial and hardly worth mentioning. We still have challenges and problems, just like everyone else. But we have already faced our worst day, and we know we can survive most anything that comes along.

One of the things I notice within myself is the ability to empathize with people in a way I could never do before. Here in our community, the local funeral director calls on me when he has need of a minister to conduct a funeral for a family who does not have a pastor.

When I'm invited to step into the sorrow of what other families are going through, I find myself grieving with them. Quite often I'm asked to conduct the funeral for families who have experienced the death of a child. These are especially difficult, because they take me back to my original sorrow. These occasions often mean I'm officiating at a funeral in the very same chapel where my son's body lay. And yes, I still feel the pain when I walk into that chapel. But it's getting better. When the families know that I, too, have lost a child, there's an instant connection, and I feel as though Buelah and I have become guides for those who are just starting their journeys through the grief jungle.

There's something else I recognize as a change in myself. In my earlier years as pastor, I always tried to be sympathetic with those who were grieving, but I'm sure I kept them at an emotionally safe distance, hoping I would not get the "disease" they had. I did all that was necessary, but no more. These days I'm not afraid to embrace the grief of other people and face it with them.

A few years ago I was making hospital calls when my

cell phone rang and my secretary told me one of our outstanding college students had died in an accident while returning home for spring break from the university she attended. When I received this news, I rushed to the home of the bereaved parents and made my way into the house. Several other people were there, and someone told me the father was upstairs in his bedroom.

I quickly walked up the stairs and into the bedroom, where I found him in his bed, on his side in a fetal position. There are no words in the English language that can help me describe the pain I witnessed when I saw him. He looked as though he had been shot and was taking his final breaths as he held his chest and screamed out from the depths of his soul. I instantly recognized that painful, primal sound that's heard only when the soul has been deeply wounded. It sounded much like the sounds I made when I discovered the body of my dead son.

Other men were standing around the bed trying to offer words of consolation. When I arrived in that room, the only thing I could do was join him in his bed of sorrow and wrap my arms around him. I still remember how his whole body shook as I held him tightly and cried with him. Before Denny's death, I would have been one of those standing close, but not too close. Now I instinctively move toward the broken heart.

There's another way in which my son's death has

changed me: my theology has changed. I mentioned that there were many times when I felt as though God had abandoned me. I borrowed the words of Jesus when He cried out from the Cross, "My God, My God, why have you forsaken me?" Not only did I feel God had forsaken me, but I also felt it was useless to pray or continue on with my spiritual exercises.

These days things are different, and I see God in a different light and with a different perspective. Looking back over this span of 17 years, I've asked myself an important question: *If I had suddenly died during this time when I was disappointed and even angry with God, where would I be spending eternity?* As mentioned previously, prior to losing Denny I would not have hesitated to answer that question by saying I would have gone straight to hell.

I suppose my concept of God was conditioned somewhat by the religious environment I grew up in as a child. I have always been in and around the church crowd. My parents became Christians a year before I was born, and we were always in church—Sunday morning, Sunday night, midweek prayer service, revivals too. Dad and Mom had a family altar, and we listened to the scriptures read each evening, and everyone prayed before going to bed. I heard thousands of sermons, several of which portrayed God as a celestial policeman, watching my every move, just waiting for the moment when I might mess up so He could write me a ticket and haul me off to jail. I don't recall hearing many sermons in my childhood about the grace of God.

I recall sitting on the church pew when my feet could not reach the floor, listening to Christians stand and share their testimonies. Probably all of these experiences combined together helped to fashion my concept of God. I viewed God as one who loved me but only in a conditional way. So as long as I toed the line and kept everything as it should be, I would be loved and accepted. Now, after going through my personal Gethsemane, I see it differently. Let me explain by telling about a special encounter.

A few years ago my wife and I were attending a district retreat for pastors and spouses in Branson, Missouri. One of our general church leaders was the special speaker, and we enjoyed what he had to say during the times he spoke to the entire group. One night after he had spoken, we had a cookie and coffee break in the café nearby.

My wife and I were seated with this leader and his wife, and we were glad to have the opportunity to visit with them because of our common sorrow. They, too, had lost a child by death, a teenage girl, so we felt a certain closeness to them. While we were drinking coffee and eating chocolate chip cookies, we started talking about our children and the way in which their deaths had changed us.

I took a chance and dared to tell him about my "shift in theology," about my changing view of God. I told him about my anger toward God and how disappointed and hurt I had been. I told him about my prayerlessness, my lack of Bible reading, and other spiritual exercises I had neglected. I told how I had tried to be a pastor and help other people and all the while had a hidden rift with God.

Then I told him how I had asked myself what would have happened to my soul if I had died during that time. I told him that before Denny's death I would have said that my questions and anger toward God would have sent me "straight to hell." Then I swallowed hard, took a deep breath, looked straight at him, and said, "I see God differently now."

He stopped me in mid-sentence, put his kind hand on my arm, and said, "I know—I know. I feel the same as you do." I looked into his face and saw the eyes of compassion, of someone who knew what I had been through. He didn't need to say anything more. His words of compassion touched my soul at a very deep level, and I felt something of what Peter felt when he was restored that day on the seashore after denying Jesus three times.

If I had been allowed to finish the sentence in which he stopped me, I would have said, "Now I believe God knew the depth of pain and suffering I was going through—He knew the awful despair and depression I was enduring. And, if I had died during that span of time, I believe He would have welcomed me home, would have thrown His arms around me and whispered into my ear, "I know—I know. Welcome home. Now, go look for your son, because he's looking for you."

These days I see God as one who is compassionate toward us, even when life has knocked the hope out of us. I find great comfort from the psalmist, who said, "The LORD is close to the brokenhearted and saves those who are crushed in spirit" (Ps. 34:18).

As I come to the end of this book, my prayer is that you'll find the hope to go on and face the future, that you'll experience this grace that we do not deserve, and that you'll one day allow this unspeakable tragedy to be used by God to help others along the way.

As we do this together, we will not allow our child's death to be the final word here. Out of the ashes of our tragedy will come a new thing that will bring blessing and healing to others.

Dennis L. Apple is on the pastoral staff at College Church of the Nazarene in Olathe, Kansas. Dennis has started numerous support groups and counsels couples and individuals who grieve the death of a child. In the church were he serves, Dennis oversees recovery and support groups, senior adult ministry, and hospital visitation. Dennis and his wife, Buelah, live in Olathe, Kansas. They have one adult son, Andrew.

You may contact Dennis Apple at Firstof1019@gmail.com.

Dennis and Buelah Apple

Denny Apple
1972-1991

Andrew Apple

comfort and support for a grieving heart

Holidays are difficult to face when you're grieving. Days of celebration are now marred by unpredictable emotions and an intensified sense of loss.

This compassionate book offers illustrations, insights, and words of comfort to help lessen the pain and heartache you expect to feel during the holidays. With keen perception, understanding, and empathy, author and grief-counselor Harold Ivan Smith helps you acknowledge your grief and learn to let God transform the season into a time of grace and healing.

A Decembered Grief
Living with Loss While Others are Celebrating
ISBN: 978-0-8341-1819-5